End

Dr. Marvin Gorman has become a Father in the Faith to me and my family. He is an Icon of Faith and Wisdom to tens of thousands of men and women in ministry today. Without question, Gods seal of approval on this great man's life is obvious in the many miracles and salvations in his current ministry. I have been blessed by God to have Dr. Marvin Gorman in my life.
--Dr. Sam Kaunley, Senior Pastor, *The Sanctuary of Hope* in Branson, Missouri

Thirty years ago Marvin Gorman became my client, later became my friend and today is my Spiritual Mentor. Reverend Gorman introduced me to the empowerment of "Holy Spirit" on June 21, 2004 and my life has never been the same.

He was a divine appointment in my life and has been a blessing to Julie and me. This book gives revelation to so many who have been bound up for years, but can now be free.
--Hunter Lundy, Attorney, Author & Christ Follower

"My Papa's teachings on Inner Healing have literally changed my life. In fact, I do not know one person who doesn't need these teachings. I strongly recommend this book to anyone and everyone. I feel blessed to have him as my grandfather."
--Sharah Gorman McGuinness, Granddaughter
Long Island, New York

For over forty-five years I have watched YHVH use Pastor Marvin Gorman to release the captives and equip believers with his teaching skill and insight. YHVH has used him powerfully in my life. I highly recommend this book.
--Marshall Carl Rice, Attorney, Shreveport, Louisiana

"The Apostle Paul points out that we have many teachers, but few fathers. (1 Corinthians 4:15) My friend Dr. Marvin Gorman is a true apostolic father in the faith. His decades of self-less service to the King has produced much fruit that remains.

This book is 'a treasure trove' of discipleship material developed over many years, and much of it through personal experience that will transform your life. I encourage you to take full advantage of Pastor Marvin's fatherly counsel within these pages."
--Eddie Smith, president, *U.S. Prayer Center*, Houston, Texas

CONQUER YOUR PAST
through
INNER HEALING

By Marvin Gorman
with Gaye Lisby

Published in the United States of America

Foundation for Human Helps
1440 State Highway 248, Suite Q167
Branson Missouri 65616

7710-T Cherry Park Dr, Ste 224
Houston, TX 77095
713-766-4271

Paperback: 978-1-68411-100-8

Hardcover: 978-1-68411-128-2

OTHER BOOKS BY MARVIN GORMAN

ANSWERS FOR THE FAMILY

CALLED TO VICTORY

HOW TO STOP SMOKING

HOW YOU CAN KNOW AND OBEY GOD'S VOICE

I MET A MAN

OBEDIENCE-YOUR KEY TO GOD'S BEST

ONE FAMILY UNDER GOD

OVERCOMING FEAR

SACRIFICE OF PRAISE

SET FREE

SLAIN IN THE SPIRIT

THE CRY OF MY HEART

THE MASTER MENTOR

THE NEW ORLEANS STORY

THE PATH TO DEEPER LIFE

THE ROAD TO REPENTANCE

UNLOCK THE DOOR

WOULD YOU BE FREE FROM YOUR BURDEN OF SIN?

YOU CAN BE FILLED WITH THE SPIRIT

Table of Contents

Dedication

I thank my wife, Virginia, who supported me as I conquered my past through inner healing.

My heartfelt thanks to her also for her time and effort in editing this book.

CHAPTER ONE:
PATHWAY TO INNER HEALING

"Is there no balm in Gilead? Is there no physician there? Why then is not the health of the daughter of my people recovered?" Jeremiah asked. *"Go up to Gilead and take balm,"* he encouraged his people (Jeremiah 8:22, 46:11). The same Holy Spirit who spoke through Jeremiah centuries ago is still encouraging us today to "take balm" and be healed. It is not God's will for His people to be bound by things from their past. Isn't it time for you to enter into the richness of this truth?

Inner healing is one of the greatest needs in the Christian church today. Wounds of the soul and spirit, if left untreated and unhealed, will keep a Christian brother or sister from carrying out the will of God in his or her life. Ultimately, it doesn't matter how the wound was created; it only matters that the person becomes healed. An old African-American Spiritual exhorts,

> There is a balm in Gilead
> To make the wounded whole;
> There is a balm in Gilead
> To heal the sin sick soul.
> Sometimes I feel discouraged,
> And think my work's in vain,
> But then the Holy Spirit
> Revives my soul again.

Perhaps you've been discouraged. Life hasn't turned out the way you thought it would. Now you're looking for a change. You may not be able to change everything about your life, but you can change one thing. That one thing is you. Conquering your past with inner healing will bring about this transformation and release you to become who you were created to be.

Those who do not attend to the healing of soul and spirit often become a danger to themselves, their families and their churches. How often Christians are dismayed to realize that they have done to someone else what once had been done to them! If they do not seek healing for their wounded soul, they will inevitably do it again. Jesus not only came to redeem the spirit, but also to redeem the soul. The mind, will and emotions, this complex human soul, is an important factor concerning how we relate to Jesus Christ, to our fellow believers and to other human beings.

Jesus said, *"The truth shall make you free."* Some folks quote, "The truth shall set you free," but Jesus said it will *"make"* you free. It will manufacture you into a free person. Those who have suffered wounds, hurts, disappointments and distresses often find they have become someone they hardly recognize anymore. Do you have the sense that you are not who you used to be? Do you feel like you are not who you want to be? The troubles and trials of life may have made you someone else. However, the truth that Jesus Christ brings can make you free to become who you really were created to be.

The truth in you makes you free when that truth is given the opportunity to function as God meant it to function. You must face the truth, then receive truth and let it work in you. I'm not talking about the truth about the other person, but the truth about yourself. Your freedom depends upon you and your relationship with God. It does not depend on others or your circumstances. Where you are does not prevent you from being free, because in a sense, freedom is a state of mind. It is a place where the mind has accommodated the truth of Jesus Christ, and what He has done for you so your will and your emotions can begin to act in accordance with that truth.

I have been dealing with many wounded people while ministering the gospel of Jesus Christ for more than six decades. Some folks easily came into the truth while others fought against and ultimately rejected the truth. How they responded to the truth determined the level of peace they had, the quality of their life and the quality of life others connected to them enjoyed. Some years ago I had the great delight to minister to a man whose name was Larry. He responded to the truth in such a way his life was totally transformed. I'll let Larry tell his testimony.

We walked into the office and shut the door. Pastor Gorman smiled at me and said, "Larry, what kind of problems are you facing in life?"

I sat for a moment with my head down. Then I heard myself say, "Well, I'm a drunk, a gambler, a thief, a liar, a whoremonger—I'm everything bad. As a matter of fact, I'm really contemplating suicide. If I wasn't such a coward, I would have already done it."

If my words shocked him, Pastor Gorman didn't show it, but I could see tears in his eyes. He opened a big, black book and handed it to me. "I want you to read First John 1:9," he said.

So I read, "If we confess our sins, God is faithful and just to forgive our sins and to cleanse us from all unrighteousness." He had me read it again, and again, this time putting my name in place of "we" and "us."

But, Pastor Gorman, you don't understand. It would take me two days to confess all my sins.

"Oh, no, Larry," he said. "God already knows every one of your sins. All you have to do is confess that you are a sinner and you want forgiveness." Then he shared with me another verse — Revelation 3:20, 'Behold, I stand at the door and knock: if any man hears my voice, and opens the door, I will come in to him, and will sup with him, and he with me.'

"The Lord is just outside your heart's door, Larry. But He is a perfect gentleman and He will never force His way in until you open the door. Do you want to let Jesus into your heart today? Would you like to pray?"

I said, "I don't know how to pray." So he had me get down on my knees and lift up my hands in surrender to God, and he led me in a prayer. I began to cry and so did he. It was so beautiful. All I heard were soothing words of forgiveness. I began to shake and tremble all over. When I got up, I told Pastor Gorman that I felt so different, so light, like a feather in the soft spring air.

He looked at his watch and said, "Praise God, you're two minutes old! You've been born again and you are a new person. All *of your sins are forgiven. If you died today, they would open the books in Heaven and say, 'Here's Larry, born again today. There is not a sin on his record. He is completely forgiven'."*

I walked out of church with Pastor Gorman's words ringing in my ears—"There is not a sin on his record. He is completely forgiven" (Gorman, The Road to Repentance).

If you are a Christian, you can rejoice because you possibly have a testimony similar to Larry's. One day the stain of sin seemed too great, and the next day you were born again, completely new, and completely forgiven. In the beginning, life seemed magically perfect. You seemed to supernaturally float above the troubles of life. You were light as a feather. Clean was the best feeling you had felt in a long time.

As time went on, the euphoria of your salvation experience began to wane and you were left to do as we all must do—work out your own salvation. Situations and circumstances of life tried to rob you of your faith in God. Loved ones wounded you. Church members misused you, misunderstood you and abandoned you. Your family members fell among the thorns of life and were torn and injured. Disease, sickness and death came to destroy. Memories of past abuses and emotional traumas began to surface. Life did not turn out the way you thought it would. Now you're reading this book and looking fine on the outside, but in anguish on the inside. You are walking the Christian walk, and beginning to understand that we are both spirit and soul in this carnal body. That is the struggle. Oh, that feather-light spirit felt wonderful after your sins were washed away, but now you are left to the dutiful walk of faith that calls on you to discover healing for your wounded soul.

"What kind of problems are you facing in life?" I had asked Larry. What I love about his testimony is that instead of saying, "My wife does this," or "my kids do that," or "my mother-in-law won't do this," Larry owned the problem by saying, "I am..." The minute he began to own the problem, he entered into the solution.

He embraced the whole truth about his life. He embraced the truth about what kind of man he had been, and then he embraced the truth about what kind of man he could become. The truth made him free. He was a drunk, a gambler, a thief, a liar, a whoremonger—everything bad. However, that wasn't the end of his story. Life and his own sinful choices had caused him to become someone he barely recognized. Entering into the truth of Jesus Christ was his first and most glorious step to becoming who he was truly designed to be. He was designed to be a loving husband and father, a good provider and protector and a faithful and productive citizen of his church and his community. When he got down on his knees and lifted his hands, Larry moved into the truth and was being manufactured into a free man.

Some Christians tell me when they were born again all things became new; therefore, they do not need to talk about their problems. They refuse to consider any thoughts about inner healing. It is absolutely true that all things became new, but your mind, will and emotions were not automatically erased when you accepted Jesus Christ into your life. The opportunity or potential for you to move into new things had been made, but you were the one who had to choose to move into these new things. Some Christians can walk the pathway to inner healing alone by digging into the Word of God and applying it faithfully and truthfully to their own heart. Sometimes, however, the wounded soul requires help from mature and trusted Christian workers.

Jesus Christ came to pay the ransom for all. Yet, not all are ransomed. By faith, we must choose to move into the salvation He has provided for us. Look around you. One glance at the nightly news proves that not all have moved into salvation although Jesus has provided salvation for all. In the same way, soul renewal has to be moved into by faith. This is the essence of inner healing. Inner healing is not some mystical thing. It is a real and necessary process for sincere Christians.

Some Christians say, "I just don't want to talk about my issues." That is the same as saying you don't want to face your issues. "It may uncover who I truly am and I just don't want to deal with it!" you may be secretly thinking. But the truth is that if you are going to have wholeness, a free, fulfilling and overcoming life, you must be willing for healing to take place within you. You may carry on with a persona that tries to convince people you are trouble-free, yet your life may be falling apart around your ears while you are busy telling yourself and others that you "don't want to talk about it."

I am reminded of the woman I ministered to who had been married five times. She told me the many problems each of her husbands had. She went to great lengths to fill me in on every one of them. Finally, I looked at her and said, "Forgive me for pointing out the obvious, but it appears that you were the common denominator in each equation." She needed to face some issues and get honest with herself.

When you decide to face your issues, do not think that just because you confess your problem it is automatically solved. A man who attended my church accidentally backed his car into mine. He came and confessed what had happened. I appreciated that fact and told him so. However, my car still needed to be repaired. Of course we called his insurance company, and they got busy making the claim, getting the estimates done and having the car repaired. He confessed and I promptly forgave, but still I needed to have my car repaired.

Some folks think that confession is all there is to coming into the truth. Confession is only the first step. All too often, confession only relieves the soul of the pressure of the sin or trouble which was confessed. Don't get me wrong, confession is a great first step. Souls seeking inner healing need to talk about it. They need to confess the problem. However, they need to move on from confession into the reality of fixing the problem. They need to be willing to stay in the process until they are fully healed.

One of the critical keys to inner healing is learning how to properly identify the problem. After that, it is much easier to construct a plan for freedom. You don't want a patch job. You want to be free, totally free. However, you cannot be free from something you do not know to be a problem. Often we are the worst at learning to identify our own problems. How many of you have ever been strutting around in fine clothes, figuring you look real nice when someone says, "Do you know you have a tear in your clothes? Do you know you have a spot on the seat of your pants?" You thought you were all dressed up. The front looked nice, but the problem is you didn't turn around. You may look nice, but you ought to see yourself walking away! Do you see that you must learn to identify the problem? That's hard to do from your own limited perspective.

My mother-in-law was a seamstress. At times she noticed there was something wrong with what I wore. Sweetly she would mention, "Marvin, did you notice one of those trouser legs is too long?" She was always checking me out. Oh, I loved her and she loved me! She did it because she loved me. She could identify the problem, but better than that, there was no problem she identified that she could not repair. That is a wonderful picture of the Holy Spirit in our lives. If we listen, He will identify our problem, and there is no problem He cannot help us fix. What's your problem? Are you brave enough to ask the Holy Spirit? Are you courageous enough and humble enough to accept the help He desires to bring?

Perhaps you feel your problem is anger. Usually what is first identified is not the problem; it is a symptom of a deeper problem. How do you begin to deal with that? Have you ever noticed the good dessert you just ate was the best you ever had? Tomorrow you might say the same thing about a different dessert. The reason is because that dessert is what you are dealing with at the moment. What will it be next week or next month? The negative emotion you are feeling right now may not be your problem, but merely a symptom of the problem. It's just that it is fresh on your mind like that most recent dessert.

You have to find that fuel source inherent in the problem. If you strike a match and lay it on the floor, it would probably just go out. However, if you add fuel then the flame could become big enough to burn down a building. Anyone can have a flash of fear. If you almost get hit by a car, you can be sure fear will flare, but usually it goes away. However, if there is fuel, it causes that fear to stay. Don't just assume what you are feeling now is your real problem. You may need to dig deeper.

Fear may be causing depression, which began because you may have become jealous. Jealous people often go into depression. This invariably results in fear. Some Christians become so depressed they lose their will to live, curl up in bed, and try to wish the world away. The symptom is depression, but jealousy was the deeper issue. Jealousy is usually caused by a deep-seated sense of insecurity, which is another version of fear. Insecurity is the fear that you are never enough. If I was insecure about my relationship with my wife, I would be very insecure about letting her out of my sight. What an awful way to live! A jealous person is miserable and makes others miserable too.

A man may be a Christian, yet be consumed by jealousy. Maybe his wife is very loyal so why is he feeling such jealousy? The reason is because he is insecure. He does not feel adequate in some way. He may be handsome enough and smart enough, yet he begins to feel he is worthless. The devil works hard to make accusations. He sends lying thoughts to produce jealousy. The truth of the matter is that it is not the wife's problem. It is the husband's problem.

Jealousy causes many marriages to go on the rocks, especially if one of the mates has remarkable ability. The other one feels threatened. If they don't recognize and repent of their jealousy, the next thing you know, they will begin to nag at each other, making slurs or catty comments. They start acting defensively and become hostile. They feel worthless and pick a fight. What are they fighting? They are fighting with their own feelings of worthlessness. Jealousy is the problem.

Suppose, for instance, it was the husband who was jealous. If this troubled man accepts the truth that the problem began with his own jealousy, and then repents, the Lord will show him the root was in his insecurities and feelings of worthlessness. Then, if he submits those feelings to God in order to be healed, he will notice his self-worth begin to grow. When he begins to feel secure again, he can stop his verbal gouging, which throws a gloom over everybody in the house all because he will not identify his own feelings of worthlessness and submit them to God.

Fear is a terrible problem that comes from many sources. Perhaps someone around you is a fearful individual. When you are around them fear tries to attack you. When God told Gideon to form an army in order to defeat the enemies of Israel, why did He tell Gideon to send the fearful home? Fear contaminates. Fear will affect good soldiers. Perhaps words spoken by someone close to you caused you to fear. Accusations thrown out during the process of a relationship breaking apart or a divorce can create a storehouse of feelings of worthlessness. This often produces fear. That storehouse has to be emptied by the Word of God. Those thoughts have to be uprooted and replaced with the truth.

Becoming healed in your inner man takes effort, consistent effort. Some people don't want to do the work involved with inner healing. They just want their pastor to pray for them. Prayer is wonderful. In fact, the Apostle Paul urged us to always pray. Ministers should pray for their flock, yet even a fervent prayer prayed by the most faithful minister will not keep a person if he is not anchored in the truth. Your pastor can lay hands on you and pray, yet that alone will not bring the cure. Even counseling will not move a person to victory unless that person takes truth, accepts it, and applies it rigorously to his thought life.

One man went to the doctor and said, "I did what you told me and things got bad again." The doctor asked, "Did you take all the medicine I gave you to get the infection out?" The man admitted he did not. He only took a couple of doses, then felt better, so he stopped taking his medicine. What happened? The infection got worse!

The truth has to be continually applied until you are totally, completely restored. You have to make it your mission. How will you know when you are restored? The thing that once bothered you won't bother you anymore. How do I know my upset stomach is cured? The answer is when I can eat anything and my stomach doesn't bother me anymore. Until that day comes, you must continually apply truth to your heart.

Too many Christians are sick in their inner being because they have held grudges from their childhood years into their mature years. During my ministry I have counseled with men and women, couples as well as singles. Most don't want to go back and deal with what happened to them in their childhood. Until that is dealt with you can clean up all you want to, but you won't have victory. Some people never deal with the past. Instead, they just get another wife or husband. They should begin to consider, "What is wrong with me?" They should consider how grudges held from their past control their future.

One time my wife and I went overseas and while we were gone our electricity went off. Our freezer and fridge defrosted and everything inside spoiled. Oh, the odor! We scrubbed and cleaned. We scrubbed again and sprayed the inside with deodorizer. Then, we cleaned the whole thing again. After a time, the stench was almost gone. With a little more elbow grease we finally had our appliances back. Liken this to your life. Perhaps there is anger, bitterness, hatred, jealousy, and strife working in you. That is what is coming out. It may have been there since you were eight years old, but now you are 58 and almost completely filled up with spoiled rottenness. You must pull everything out and get down to the business of scrubbing.

You must get it all out or it will make an odor that contaminates everything. Perhaps you ripped someone with your tongue. The devil makes it bigger than what it was and he stops you in your walk with God. Instead, why not go back and deal with the issue? Good counselors can help you go back and find where the root of the problem began, even if it is in your childhood. It may hurt. You may shed a lot of tears. It is true that someone else may have initiated the hurt. Someone may have sinned against you, but where you failed was by holding onto it and allowing your life experiences to add to it. Who have you hurt as a result of your being wounded?

Once, a lady from another church nagged me for counseling. I finally relented and set up an appointment with her. She brought a letter from her pastor. She told me, "I have demons and I've come for you to cast them out of me." I went along with this by asking, "What kind?" She unzipped her purse and took out a list. She said, "I have twenty-nine." "Who told you this," I asked. She said her prayer group told her about them and even what their names were. I just sat there amazed. I finally told her, "Lady, the Holy Spirit doesn't let you name what you cannot cast out!" We put the list aside.

We eventually found out her root problem was her intense hatred for her step-mother. She hated the old gal! She hoped she was in hell. What if the step-mother was viciously mean? It doesn't matter. She was dead and her step-daughter was sitting in my office eaten up with bitterness and hatred.

You might say, "You don't know my mother, grandmother, or my aunt!" Or you might say, "I'm like this because that's the way my daddy was." You try to justify the fights and the violence, but that just means you aren't trying to get over it any more than he was. The answer to your anger is not going to your room, closing the door and screaming, kicking, punching and venting. You need to be emptied. Maybe you have been hurt by something someone said. While you are letting that eat on you, he's over there eating steak and not thinking two thoughts about you. Be careful what you give your soul over to.

When Larry came to me that day and was wonderfully born again, he embarked on a journey that took him through some joyous places and through some hard places. He had to go home and make things right with his wife and children. He had to earn their trust by being truthful and sincere in everything. He had to let the Holy Spirit examine his heart and clean out all the cabinets and closets of the past. He had to face his history and uncover anything that might try to drag him back into the life of sin.

He was truly born again when he prayed with me that day. If he had died that night, he would have gone straight to heaven. He was as clean as a newly washed babe, but his soul carried a residue of his past. That was the place he would have to focus some attention if he wanted to grow in Christ, and grow in relationship with his family and the church.

Some Christians are so spiritual they check their brains at the door of the church. They pretend they don't have a mind, will or emotions to influence their spirit life. They are living in a deception that will eventually trap them in sin. Our soul is a vital part of our relationship with Jesus Christ. A healthy soul is a healthy place for Jesus Christ to be glorified and for Him to carry on the work of the Kingdom of God.

Perhaps you've been born again, but never dealt with the issues that make your soul sickly and weak. Journey on this pathway to inner healing and discover what has kept you from thriving in your spiritual walk. Let the Holy Spirit search your innermost being and show you how to overcome the power of the wounded soul. I have ministered to almost every type of wound imaginable, yet I have not found a single person who could not be fully healed if he diligently applied himself to walk the pathway to inner healing. You can be healed. I know it for a fact. I have walked this pathway myself.

CHAPTER TWO:
REPENTANCE AND FORGIVENESS— THE AXIS OF FAITH

Human nature is no good at either repentance or forgiveness. If left to our own devices, we avoid both at all costs. Sadly, the cost is all too often paid by wounding other souls. Our carnal nature rebels against repentance and forgiveness because both require a humility that only the Spirit possesses. A Christian must decide to leave his own carnal nature in order to take up the nature of Christ. The flesh rails against the thought, but repentance and forgiveness are the axis of faith.

The "Blessing of Repentance" is a powerful technique that helps to remove each layer of the problem in your life until the root can be clearly seen and properly destroyed. Think of it like peeling an onion. Perhaps you believe fear is your problem. Begin by acknowledging to God in prayer that you have this issue. Acknowledge that it is there and that it shouldn't be there. "Lord, I am filled with fear and I know it is not your will for me." Then begin to repent of the fear. "But I didn't do anything wrong!" you may protest. The truth is by living in fear you are doing something wrong. God didn't give you a spirit of fear, but of power and of love and of a sound mind. So this spirit did not come from God and you are not moving in the power, love and a sound mind He has given you. It's time to repent. Remember, this is not about assigning fault or blame; instead, this is about getting to the root of the problem in your life that is keeping you from living a rich and full life.

Realize it is a blessing to repent. Repentance is not a dreadful, terrible thing. If you truly love the Lord it will be a joy to repent and set your heart right with him. "Lord, I repent that I have let fear rule my life. Show me what I am afraid of and fill me with the power to overcome this obstacle." If you are sincere and consistent, the Holy Spirit will begin to reveal things to you.

Shortly, you may begin to understand your trust in the Lord is not strong, so that is why you are still afraid. You can run away and hide from this fact or you can begin to let the Holy Spirit move inside of you. If you will repent of your lack of trust, you may discover something else. "Lord, I repent because I am always afraid. I am realizing I do not trust you. Please forgive me for not trusting in you. Your Holy Scripture tells me you are always faithful, trustworthy and true. I choose to believe the scriptures instead of what I am feeling at this moment. Forgive me and fill my heart with trust in you." You will begin to feel growth in your level of trust. Your confidence in your relationship with Jesus will begin to flourish as fear begins to fade. Now the Holy Spirit is really working in you and you want Him to keep on working.

The Holy Spirit may show you that the mistrust you have toward the Lord is because your earthly father could not be trusted. Perhaps he was creeping into your room at night to do unspeakable things to you. Perhaps he was abusing your mother in front of you. Maybe he was an alcoholic who drank up all the money so there was never enough for you to have your basic needs met. Your early years were filled with painful incidents that caused you to mistrust your father. When you were born again, you unwittingly transferred this mistrust into your relationship with God as your Father. You didn't feel confident in His love. You didn't feel like He was trustworthy. Instead, you always felt fearful, like He might hurt you or let you down. You learned to hide your fear, but deep down you were always terrified that someone would find out how fearful you really were. Because you began to repent, all this started coming to the surface.

At this point, if you get sidetracked by the "blame game" you will slow down your healing process, and perhaps even derail it altogether. The bottom line is that perhaps the whole mess was your father's fault. That may be true, but that doesn't cure anything. What brings the cure is if you continue in the process of repenting so you can be fully healed and fully delivered from the fear that was strangling you for so long.

Go back to the Lord and repent that you transferred your mistrust to Him when actually it was mistrust you had for your earthly father. Ask Jesus to wash your mind, will and emotions from the residue of the hurtful actions that destroyed your trust. When you do, the Lord will begin to gently wash away those wounds and rebuild in you a desire to trust again. He may bring trustworthy Christians into your life to speak to you and build you up. He may begin to cause others to trust in you and look to you for help. He will grow trust in you if you let Him. When you practice repentance and search the scriptures, it is like lifting the lid from a pot and seeing what boils underneath.

The Christian man who suffers from bouts of anger and jealousy should use repentance to get to the bottom of what troubles him. He may have first thought his problem was depression. If he begins to repent of his depression, he may discover he really suffers from a root of anger. The Holy Spirit may take him and show him that anger resulted from his mother rejecting and abandoning him so that he began to feel worthless. He must begin to repent that he let those feelings of worthlessness take him to a place of anger and rage. Then God can replace those feelings of worthlessness with feelings of value.

The Holy Spirit will send people to him to tell him how valuable he is to the Kingdom of God. The Word of God will fill him, and minister value and self-worth to him. He will realize that God's eye is on him. God always listens and cares for him. Soon the anger will abate because it is not fueled by those negative emotions from his damaging past. After a time, this brother will realize the depression has lifted because the anger and feelings of worthlessness are gone.

Perhaps cold-heartedness is the problem you've identified today. How do you deal with that in order to find out if anything else is behind it? The answer is simply through repentance. That is why I called it the "Blessing of Repentance." You might pray, "Father, forgive me that I am cold-hearted. I cannot seem to feel or care about the sorrows of others. My compassion is gone." Then go to the scriptures and study all the verses on compassion. As different

28

scriptures prompt something in your heart; keep repenting because there is something inside you that is fueling that cold-heartedness.

You may discover that you have not truly forgiven your husband for committing adultery against you. You may find that caused you to be cold-hearted and indifferent toward him and toward others. You stayed in the marriage, but you locked up your heart and became mechanical in your dealings with people. If you will repent, the Lord will heal your heart and fill it with the warmth of His love again. You will find you can love out of the reservoir of His love. Your cold-heartedness toward your husband and toward others will disappear.

I am convinced that many of the problems that exist in the Body of Christ today stem from the fact people have never truly repented. They have never honestly dealt with the contents of the deep recesses of their own heart. They refuse to wait before God and let Him search them out until they literally hate the thing that has caused them this difficulty. I do not mean they should hate the person who has caused them difficulty. I mean they should hate the sin in their own lives so much that it literally makes them sick to think about it.

Christians must live a lifestyle of repentance. We must repent daily. We must diligently study the Word of God. The more you study the scriptures, the more you will see the areas which the Holy Spirit wants to help scrub out of your life. By looking at yourself in the mirror of the Word, you will begin to view yourself truthfully. The more truth you have the more truth you will want. The more truth you receive, the easier it will be to repent. You will receive joyfully the molding and shaping of your life that is produced by the truth of the scriptures because you will see more clearly who you can become.

Have you ever seen a little toddler mimicking his father or mother? He is well on his way to becoming what he is beholding. Behold the Word of God. Meditate on it. Enjoy it. Let it enrich your spirit and soul. If you haven't eaten all day and suddenly you smell homemade bread, there is nothing that tastes better than a warm slice of yeasty bread with rich, creamy butter. The Word of God will become just that satisfying and enjoyable to you the more you read, study and then respond to the Word of God in repentance.

In Joel 2:12, the prophet depicts the horrible judgments to come on Israel because of their rebellious sins. *"Now, therefore,"* says the Lord, *"Turn to me with all your heart, with fasting, with weeping and with mourning. In this passage, turn means, "keep on turning to the Lord."* Keep on until you are totally restored. Turn and keep turning because of the security you have in your relationship with the Lord. Your transformation won't happen all at once. However, if you will work every day with steady effort, you can be totally restored.

Have you ever bought something that had to be restored? You owned it but it wasn't restored. Just because you are saved does not mean you have been restored. One young man got saved in one of my meetings. He was standing at the back of the altar area when he shouted, "Preacher, that was a hell of a sermon you preached today!" He was saved, but his language was not yet restored. Turn and keep turning. Repent and keep repenting. The "Blessing of Repentance" is a powerful way to cleanse your inner being.

Make a habit of repenting daily. Years ago the Lord spoke to me and said, "A day without repentance is like eating every meal from the same dirty plate you used for breakfast." I learned to develop a lifestyle of repentance. I learned to ask the Lord to change my heart toward a person, situation or my painful past. If you repent and earnestly ask God to purify you, if you pour your heart out in that manner to God, if you truly get down to business with your Bible study, in a short time you will be a different person. Restoration is possible because Jesus gave His life for it.

How will you know when you are totally free? One time the Lord took me to Psalm 51 and showed me something so vital. King David understood that until he saw himself as having sinned against God and only God, he hadn't reached the bottom of his problem. David said, "Against you and you only have I sinned!" What did he mean? When you come to a certain point in your journey of repentance, you will understand that ultimately it was not the other person, or the church, nor even your family that you sinned against. Your sin was against God. All sin is ultimately against God.

Remember what happened to Peter after he denied the Lord? Jesus just looked at him and Peter ran out and bitterly wept. Did he weep because he lied? No, he wept because he failed Jesus. He hurt Jesus. So much of what we call repentance is just asking someone for forgiveness or worse yet, just saying we are sorry. It is vital to realize what our sin does to Jesus. We fail Him. Repentance restores our spirit and causes us to become sensitive to Jesus again. When we behave in such a way that offends or hurts Him, we feel sorrow that quickly moves us to repentance. We should want to bring glory and honor to Him and give Him cause to rejoice over us. We will never be totally free until we realize that our sins are against our Savior.

The axis of the Christian faith is two-dimensional. It is both repentance and forgiveness. We need to repent, but we also need to forgive just as much as we need to repent. Often it is much harder to forgive than it is to repent. We want to be forgiven, but we do not readily want to forgive. Jesus commanded us to forgive so that we can be forgiven.

Corrie ten Boom was a twentieth century giant of faith. This humble Dutch woman suffered horribly at the hands of Nazis for the simple crime of loving and caring for Jews. Her father, beloved sister and other family members died in German concentration camps. Miraculously, Corrie survived. Her devout moral principles were tested when, by chance, she came face to face with one of her former tormentors in 1947. The following description of that experience is excerpted from her 1971 autobiography, The Hiding Place, written with the help of John and Elizabeth Sherrill.

"It was in a church in Munich that I saw him, a balding heavy-set man in a gray overcoat, a brown felt hat clutched between his hands. People were filing out of the basement room where I had just spoken. It was 1947 and I had come from Holland to defeated Germany with the message that God forgives. And that's when I saw him, working his way forward against the others. One moment

I saw the overcoat and the brown hat; the next, a blue uniform and a visored cap with its skull and crossbones. It came back with a rush: the huge room with its harsh overhead lights, the pathetic pile of dresses and shoes in the center of the floor, the shame of walking naked past this man. I could see my sister's frail form ahead of me, ribs sharp beneath the parchment skin. Betsie, how thin you were! Betsie and I had been arrested for concealing Jews in our home during the Nazi occupation of Holland; this man had been a guard at Ravensbruck concentration camp where we were sent. "You mentioned Ravensbruck in your talk," he was saying. "I was a guard in there." No, he did not remember me. "But since that time," he went on, "I have become a Christian. I know that God has forgiven me for the cruel things I did there, but I would like to hear it from your lips as well. Fraulein," his hand came out, "will you forgive me?" And I stood there — I whose sins had every day to be forgiven — and could not. Betsie had died in that place — could he erase her slow, terrible death simply for the asking? It could not have been many seconds that he stood there, hand held out, but to me it seemed hours as I wrestled with the most difficult thing I had ever had to do. I had to do it — I knew that. The message that God forgives has a prior condition: that we forgive those who have injured us. "If you do not forgive men their trespasses," Jesus says, "neither will your Father in heaven forgive your trespasses." And still I stood there with the coldness clutching my heart. But forgiveness is not an emotion — I knew that too. Forgiveness is an act of the will, and the will can function regardless of the temperature of the heart. "Jesus, help me!" I prayed silently. "I can lift my hand; I can do that much. You supply the feeling." And so woodenly, mechanically, I thrust my hand into the one stretched out to me. And as I did, an incredible thing took place. The current started in my shoulder, raced down my arm, sprang into our joined hands. And then this healing warmth seemed to flood my whole being, bringing tears to my eyes. "I forgive you, brother!" I cried. "With all my heart!" For a long moment we grasped each other's hands, the former guard and the former prisoner. I had never known God's love as intensely as I did then."

We may never face the terrible hardships and crimes committed against us like Corrie ten Boom faced. Yet each of us has those in our lives for whom forgiveness seems an impossibility. It is only after we have faced our own necessity to repent and be forgiven that we realize how blessed it is to forgive. Jesus said, "He who has been forgiven much loves much." Soul wounds often blind us to our own need to be forgiven. We can see the glaring faults of others, but we will not look in the spiritual mirror at ourselves. If we ever do look, all too often, we raise our chins against the Holy Spirit and say, "But he did that to me..." Our unforgiveness keeps us from true repentance. And that keeps us from growing in our relationship with our Lord Jesus Christ.

Jesus required us to forgive. "How many times must we do this? Seven times?" Peter asked. He was feeling pretty good about that. Seven is a lot. Jesus looked at him and said, "Seventy times seven." Whoa! What was Jesus thinking? Are we to just stand there and let them abuse us again? That is not what Jesus was saying. He was saying that our hearts must be positioned so that forgiveness flows out easily because in a minute we will probably want it to be flowing back in our direction.

During my ministry I have discovered that it is often the most wounded Christians who repent the least. It is because they are also the ones who will forgive the least. Somehow the wound takes precedence over the truth. The person would rather stay wounded than learn to forgive.

Forgiveness is a process. Sometimes it is as much a daily act of faith as repentance. Some Christians have been injured and they should pray daily for forgiveness toward their abusers. If they would do this by faith, they would soon find the warmth of true forgiveness working in their hearts.

It is a strange spiritual truth that the more we repent, the more we can forgive, because then we see our own need for forgiveness. Forgiveness is not an easy thing, but it is a necessary thing. Many a Christian has fallen on the rocks of unforgiveness and gone back into a life of sin. They usually point to a certain person in their lives as being at fault. The truth is their unwillingness to obey the scriptures and forgive is the reason they have fallen away from God.

Corrie ten Boom said, "And I stood there — I whose sins had every day to be forgiven — and could not." Then she remembered a key point about forgiveness; just like repentance, it is an act of faith, not a feeling. "Forgiveness is not an emotion," she recounted. She remembered forgiveness is an act of the will. She chose to position her heart to obey and because of that she had a glorious moment with her Heavenly Father as well as with the man who was now her brother in Christ.

That must have been how the apostles felt the first time they met Paul. They remembered him as the zealous Pharisee who was hauling Christians out of their homes to be slaughtered. He had stood by and watched while Stephen was cruelly stoned to death. They heard by word of mouth he had been miraculously converted on the road to Damascus, but now Paul was coming to extend his hand, to ask for forgiveness, and the right hand of fellowship. How their hearts must have echoed with the screams of women and children, and the anguished cries of men as they were hauled off to their deaths! As soothing balm, the Holy Spirit brought to their remembrance the time Jesus told them to forgive. He taught them that forgiveness was a requirement of the Christian faith, not a garnish on their religious plate. They forgave Paul and admitted him to fellowship with them.

You might be arguing in your head with me now, "Yes, but in both Corrie ten Boom's case, and in Paul's case, they asked for forgiveness. My abuser has not even acknowledged his sin – much less asked for forgiveness." It is true that is the more difficult case. However, Jesus Christ was the role model for our proper response. He was brutally beaten, shamefully hung, bleeding on a cross, and taking the punishment that we deserved. Around Him the angry mob howled and screamed out false accusations. With His dying breath, He lifted Himself on His shredded feet and cried, "Father, forgive them for they do not know what they are doing."

Neither the mob, nor His torturers would ever ask for forgiveness, but He forgave anyway. He released them from the punishment they deserved. He relinquished His right to vengeance. He left them in the hands of God. They didn't know and they didn't care, but Jesus did it anyway.

Believers must remember repentance and forgiveness are the axis of Christian faith. Everything we are or ever will be revolves around these two acts of obedience. By obeying the "Blessing of Repentance," you can learn to plumb the depths of your soul and be cleansed from every weight and sin that so easily besets you. By learning to practice forgiveness as an act of your will, your very innermost being will begin to be healed.

These are not works of the flesh, but works of the Holy Spirit through our flesh. The more we repent and receive God's forgiveness, the easier it is to give forgiveness to others. Little by little we will become the Christians we were meant to be, and the Kingdom of God will be richer and healthier because of it.

CHAPTER THREE:
VICTORY THROUGH SORROW AND COMPASSION

There is no one who wants to experience sorrow during their lifetime. Sorrow, that distressed mind caused by loss, affliction or disappointment may be felt as grief, sadness or regret. No one wants to suffer loss, affliction or disappointment. No one enjoys feelings of grief, sadness or regret. Yet, if you live long enough, you are likely to have occasions to experience sorrow. Very few people would ever think of sorrow in a positive light. But, is it possible sorrow can be a blessing? How can that be possible?

Job sorrowed over his catastrophic losses. Jesus sorrowed over Jerusalem when He sat on the hillside overlooking that beloved city. He wept as He spoke prophetically concerning what would happen to Jerusalem. Isaiah records that the Messiah was a "man of sorrows, acquainted with grief." Peter sorrowed when he realized his Lord had been correct to prophesy his betrayal. He wept bitterly. David sorrowed when the prophet Nathan pointed at him and said, "Thou art the man." David's sin with Bathsheba had been uncovered. His wicked orchestration of her husband's murder had been revealed. David's heart was ripped open, and the poison of lust and power was exposed. He sorrowed. Sorrow seems like a bad thing. How is it possible then that sorrow could be a blessing?

In Jeremiah 31:19 the prophet said, *"Surely after that I was turned, I repented; and after that I was instructed I smote my thigh.*

I was ashamed even confounded because I did bear the reproach of my youth." He was confounded. He sorrowed. This verse deals with the fact that when we realize the depth of our sin and its cost paid by others and paid by Jesus, we will become very sorry for our sin. We will feel deep sadness, grief and regret. Sorrow for sin means taking sin at its depth, dealing with what it has done to us, and what it has done to others. It is that kind of sorrowing which can bring a blessing.

Peter sorrowed when he knew he had betrayed Jesus as woefully as Judas. The difference between Peter and Judas is that Judas ran away from Christ and His forgiveness, while Peter ran toward Christ and His forgiveness. Peter soon found himself wiping away bitter tears of regret. He heard his Lord say, "Peter, do you love Me? Then feed My sheep." Peter loved his Lord and agreed to feed His sheep. The Lord continued however, "Peter do you love Me? Then feed My sheep." Now Peter was thinking about things. Why was his Lord repeating Himself? The third time Jesus asked, "Peter, do you love Me? Then feed My sheep." Peter knew what Jesus was doing. By asking this question three times, Jesus was erasing the shame of Peter's three vehement denials, "I do not know Him!" Both Judas and Peter had betrayed Jesus. Judas had gone and hanged himself. Peter came back to Jesus. One sorrowed unto repentance and was restored. The other sorrowed without repentance and was destroyed.

The first thing that you should understand about sorrow is the same thing the prodigal son understood. The prodigal son came to his senses. He said, "I'm in a hog pen and my father's servants are treated better than I'm being treated."

When he came to his senses he turned. When he turned, it did not put him back into relationship with his father. For him to come back into relationship with his father, he had before him a long journey. He denounced the sin at the hog pen. He said he was through with sin, through with the world and through with all that brought him down. So he turned around, climbed out of that hog pen and said, "I'm going to my father's house. I'm going to ask my father if he will allow me to just be one of his hired servants. I will be content with that." He still had not seen his father. He had not yet approached his father, but he had denounced the old life. He got up and went back the way he came down.

How many of you know that the way back is the way you came down? To go home, you have to get back on the same street you left. You're going to pass the same houses and the same businesses. This boy came out of the hog pen, but he had to walk by everything that had tempted him and brought him to the hog pen in the first place. He walked by everything and denounced it as he went by. He became totally emptied of all that brought him down. He hated the sin and detested what he had been.

He came back to his father in humility without making any demands because he had emptied himself along the way. Jeremiah said, *"After I turned…"* In other words, he realized he was going the wrong way. He turned. The prodigal son turned. He went back the way he had come. Turn and go back the way you came. Stop trying to avoid the mess you made. Go back and lean on the strength of God to help you make it right.

Why is it important to deal with the subject of sorrow for sin when we are really trying to come to a place of inner healing? The reason is so many Christians deal with sin only in respect to how it affected them. The prodigal son could have done that as well. He could have gotten up out of the pen, washed up, sworn off the party lifestyle and gotten a job. He could have said to himself, "The sin was between me and God. I repented. God forgave. That's that." But the truth of the matter is that wasn't that. Sin affects many lives. Your sin impacted others. Your sin broke your mother's heart. You need to be restored to her. Your sin shattered your companion's life. You need to help restore them and restore your family. It is true that at the very depths of the matter your sin was against God, but the damage was far-reaching. Godly sorrow for sin should motivate you to make things right. Judas over-sorrowed and took the coward's way out. He hung himself, never facing the consequences of his sin. Peter sorrowed and stayed. He was restored and became a foundational apostle of the early church.

The Apostle Paul wrote, *"For godly sorrow produces repentance leading to salvation, not to be regretted; but the sorrow of the world produces death."* (II Corinthians 7:10) Godly sorrow changes the life and cleanses it of sin. Worldly sorrow overwhelms the soul causing death and destruction. Worldly sorrow leaves you in a grievous, emotional state without remedy. Worldly sorrow causes emotional withdrawal, numbness and emptiness. Many people in the world hide their sins from their own hearts and minds, and turn to other sins to mask their sorrows. Have you ever heard of a drunk trying to "drown his sorrows?" What does that mean? His worldly sorrow has overwhelmed his soul, and caused him to seek out destructive alcohol in order to mask the pain, hide from the consequences and ignore the fall-out.

Those who commit sexual sins are often most susceptible to ignoring the blessing of godly sorrow. Men who commit adultery may simply divorce their wife or let them file for divorce. Then they just find a new wife. They never deal with the depths of their sin. They act like it was just a momentary lapse in judgment instead of a horrendous and damaging act of betrayal. They sugar-coat their own sin, maybe even eventually going to church and praying their bland little prayer, "Bless me Father, for I have sinned," and walk out unmoved by what they have done.

True repentance means letting the realization of what you have done go deeply into your own soul, birthing within you a fervent desire to avoid that sin no matter what. You will never read about the prodigal son returning to the pig pen. He never did. He felt the full weight of what he had done. He saw the pain in his father's eyes. He tasted the goodness of being fully forgiven and fully restored, and he would never let anything steal that peaceful unity from him again.

The kind of person the Lord can help is a person with a broken and contrite heart. After you turn from your sin, you must start repenting of the things you did and who you were. You can't repent until you make up your mind you are going to give it up. You can't go home until you decide you want to go home. When you make up your mind and start toward home there must be godly sorrow for sin. Every place you go by will remind you of what you have done. This time though, it will not be a place of pleasure or frolic, but a place of pain, deep pain. Some people slide so easily back into sin because they've never let the pain of what they've done wash over them. They ignore sin and pretend it didn't happen. Once you deal with the pain of sin and what it has cost you and others, you will never want to revisit that again. Once you really let it bring forth the hurt that it has caused, you will never want to go back.

We older folks used to have space heaters to help heat our drafty houses. We knew a little something about trying to keep our toddlers safe. We built fences around those space heaters, put up barriers around them, and stood between the space heaters and the little ones. We said over and over, "Don't touch!" Some of us had kids who were headstrong and thought we might as well be saying, "Here, touch this!" Sooner or later they would. But after they touched it, every time they would see that space heater, they would reach out their little hands toward it, while staying very far back and say, "Hot! Don't touch!" What made the difference? The pain made the difference.

The reason people keep falling back into sin is they have never dealt with the pain of being set free, and the pain of watching those they hurt try to get healed. The truth is they have never really repented. They confessed. They said, "Sorry!" but they did not do an "about face!" When true sorrow for sin rests squarely on your shoulders you will never want to go back into that sin again.

Some Christians rebel against the idea of godly sorrow. They want to talk all day long about the wrongs committed against them by others. However, they want to ignore the wrongs they have done. Survivors of abuse may spend so much time thinking about the bad things other people did, they end up winking at their own sins. If someone points out the fact their healing would come about more rapidly if they dealt with their own sin, they flare up in anger and accuse others of not caring about their pain. God cares about their pain, but He also cared about their sins so much that He gave His only son to die for their sins. There has to be a personal acknowledgement of sin, and a personal sorrowing for sin.

In Zechariah 12:10, the prophet spoke, *"And I will pour on the house of David and on the inhabitants of Jerusalem the Spirit of grace and supplication; then they will look on Me whom they pierced. Yes, they will mourn for Him as one mourns for his only son, and grieve for Him as one grieves for a firstborn."* Why did God say He would pour upon them the spirit of grace? Because grace helps to mellow and strengthen you knowing that you have favor from God. Grace keeps you from over-sorrowing. Healthy sorrow, or godly sorrow, is that deep weeping and seeking God. From that position you will see that your sin did as much damage to the Lord Jesus Christ as the man who nailed the spikes into His hands and feet. You are mourning for Jesus. You are mourning for what you did to Him. You mourn for Him as you would mourn for your firstborn son who died.

Godly sorrow works repentance unto salvation. That is why I can readily say there is a blessing in sorrow. The blessing is many-fold. You are blessed because your godly sorrow has worked true repentance. You are blessed because godly sorrow causes you to place safe-guards in your life so you will never go back to that sin. Others who love you are blessed because they no longer suffer the consequences of your sin. They are blessed to have you working with them to restore what was lost. Godly sorrow is a blessing because it works true and lasting change.

Godly sorrow also works sensitive compassion. Those who have been courageous enough to feel and accept the full weight and responsibility for their sins and the damage they have done will have abundant compassion on others. When you get your life on solid ground, a sympathetic compassion begins to fill you. You know what it is like to fall into sin and disappoint someone, or even to devastate a life.

Compassion is void of the self-righteousness, which filled the Pharisees of Jesus' day. Jesus was moved with compassion for the woman caught in adultery. He confronted the self-righteous mob with a simple writing on the ground. Soon the condemned woman's accusers had vanished. "Neither do I condemn you. Go and sin no more," Jesus said. He had compassion. Because of his compassion, her life was saved and the hypocrisy of the Pharisees was exposed.

Compassion helps you realize everybody is hurting in some way. Everybody has their little red wagon to pull around. When I remember how I used to hurt, it makes me more sensitive to others. When I remember how I wanted to be treated when I was hurting, I endeavor to treat others that way. We quote the Golden Rule, "Do unto others as you would have them do unto you," but unfortunately we have trouble living it.

When my sons were young, Randy and Mark had their own interpretation of that one. I heard them and their mother having a discussion you could hear for about two blocks. It was just before the war started, and Captain Virginia was in charge of the war! I heard Mark say, "But, Mother, the Bible says, 'Do unto others as you would have them do unto you.' I know he wanted me to hit him because he hit me first!" Mark and Randy missed the point of what Jesus was teaching. What we call the Golden Rule was meant to encourage us to feel compassion, not retaliation.

Love and compassion gives you the ability to make allowances for other people's imperfections. Some people say, "Brother Gorman, I allow for other people's imperfections!" Yes, I see that. The people on this side of your house hurt you last week so you built a thirty-foot fence on that side. The ones behind you hurt you this week so you built a fence all around you. Next, you got a Doberman Pincher and put him by the gate. Then you come to church and tell me you love your neighbors, but you just can't deal with them! The truth is you don't love them and you can't deal with them because there is too much in you that you haven't dealt with yet.

Once you deal with your hurts and let Jesus heal them you remember the process you went through. You remember the pain. All of that comes back to your remembrance and you remember the merciful God who helped you through it. Then you can easily take your neighbor by the hand, loving them as God loved you, until you bring them into the ability to see their need.

When they begin to deal with their problems you know they may have all sorts of conflicting moods. Some might feel like they made it to the top of the mountain one day, but by the next day in church they're snappy and grouchy. If you're in the healing process, the person who is gently leading you down the path toward healing may soon be the object of your irritation. However, because he or she has already traveled down the pathway to healing, they should have compassion for you and should not respond to you the way you respond to them.

When I started counseling I had to realize that, as I pulled back the mask on a hurting brother or sister and took away their ability to blame someone else (before they accepted blame themselves), they would often take a shot at me. One man said he was better off before he came to see me. I told him, "I didn't make this mess. For all I know you were born a mess. You've been a mess since the first time I saw you. What we're doing is stripping down all the phoniness where we can get down to the real person." That's what has to be done. All that veneer has to be stripped away.

I have to help them denounce that before they can see themselves as they really are. Until they do they will never change. Sometimes when I'm counseling it seems like every thirty seconds I have to say, "Wait a minute, we're not dealing with them. Let's come back to the real issue. The real issue is you." I do this because I know what it is like to walk the pathway to inner healing and suddenly be afraid of being fully revealed.

In Psalms 119:59 it says, *"I thought about my ways, and turned my feet to Your testimonies."* People don't like to think on their ways. They don't like to stop and deal with who they are as an individual. I'm not talking about some sort of impersonal analyzing. I'm talking about thinking on your ways to such a degree it produces a desire to change. I have compassion on others. I encourage them to take the time to "think on their ways..." Lots of people want to think about other people's ways. They want to think about what their mean step-mother did or what their drunken father did or didn't do. They get over-anxious and fretful trying to think on everybody else's ways.

The truth is you have to deal with what is in your life now. What caused it becomes less important. If you contracted a deadly disease, would it matter who you got it from? Would it make you feel any better to know? Would it cure you to know? Absolutely not! The important thing is that you would want to be healed. In the same way, you have to look at your problems by thinking on your ways. Your ways are the only ways you can change. I have a lot more compassion when I counsel people today because I know what it's like to look for every excuse or reason for my own behavior.

Compassion also causes you to remember to deal humbly with others who have sinned. Peter could deal humbly with others because he knew the pain of sinful betrayal. In I Peter 1:3, he wrote, *"Blessed be the God and Father of our Lord Jesus Christ, who according to His abundant mercy has begotten us again to a living hope through the resurrection of Jesus Christ from the dead."* Peter opened his letter by shining his light on God's abundant mercy. Those who have experienced God's abundant mercy the most are the ones who enjoy celebrating God's abundant mercy the most.

Humility is the only way to walk in this mercy. There was a time Peter thought he had arrived at the place of spiritual preeminence. Peter received a word of knowledge, but thirty minutes later he was receiving words from the devil. Words of knowledge do not sanctify anyone. Gifts of the Spirit do not sanctify the one operating in the gifts. It is repentance and the consistent application of the Word to their life. You can minister to others in your life with compassion while recognizing that you haven't arrived. The moment you get to the point you feel you have arrived, you may fall into the pit of self-righteousness. At that point the compassion you need to minister with will vanish.

Some people have a problem with me bringing up what I did back in 1978. They might as well get used to me speaking about it because I will never forget what God did for me by His divine grace. He brought me out of the sin and shame of adultery. He cleansed me and restored my soul. He restored me to my wife and my family. He restored me to the body of Christ.

I will continue to speak about what happened because I want to remind myself that there is a devil that can and will trap me if I'm not on my guard. I also want to show every living being that it doesn't matter what hell tries to do to you. If you choose to hold onto God you can overcome. I've had preachers tell me, "Don't ever tell anyone." I decided I was not going to become a self-righteous person who pretended he had done everything right. I didn't do everything right. I'm here today by the grace of God and the grace of God only. I have the compassion to tell you the truth about myself, and encourage you with my own life so that you know you can be victorious too.

There is a point in your Christian walk where you may be called upon to show great compassion. You may find yourself mourning over, even praying with great intercession and agony, for the ones who have wronged you the most. I remember on October 11, 1987, my son, Mark, was preaching. Suddenly I was caught up in intercession so intense it seemed my heart would burst. I was in great travail and mourning. It felt like someone reached into my chest and had both hands around my heart. I was in physical pain and deep spiritual intercession. Many people gathered around me, but I was so caught up in this intercession I was only vaguely aware of them.

For nearly two hours I went through this excruciating experience of mourning and sobbing. The faces of seven people were brought before me in the Spirit, yet I could see them as clearly as if they physically stood before me. Each looked me in the eye. Then they would move and the next one would come before me. This went on until all seven passed in front of me. Then the Lord said to me, "You must forgive them."

I said, "Lord, I have. I have prayed for them. I have forgiven every one of them."

The Lord then said, "Yes, but now you must make them your friends."

I answered, "Lord, they don't want to be my friends. You know what they have done. They don't want to be my friends. Lord, they will have nothing to do with me."

The Lord patiently reiterated his request. "O.K. Lord, but you will have to help me because I don't understand."

"You must pray for them as your friends. You pray for friends differently than you pray for others. The captivity of Job was turned when he prayed for his friends," the Lord said.

Did you ever check out what kind of friends Job had? They told him he was a sinner. "If you didn't have sin in your life this would not be happening to you. You have sin in your life and you are lying about it," they accused him. Would you like to have a healing line with the first one in line being your worst enemy?

As the compassion of God works in you, you will come to a place you can mourn for the condition of the one who has treated you the worst. That experience happened to me that October. In my heart, I forgave each one of them that night. Sometime after that I made personal contacts asking for their forgiveness. Eventually God vindicated me because I forgave them and reached out my hand to be their friend. If I would have maintained vengeance in my heart toward them, I would have never been forgiven. Each of them knows that if they were to call me today and need my help I would rush to their aid. I have compassion in my heart for them although they had set themselves to destroy me and my family.

God will judge us for the way we treat those whom He allows to come into our lives. For us to be able to minister to others there must be a spirit of love and compassion on our part. If we don't stay tender and mellow then we will not receive them in love and compassion when they come. Wouldn't it be great when you get to heaven if the person who has hurt you the most walked up and said, "Thank you for loving me. It's because you showed me the love of Jesus that I'm here today." Wouldn't it be great to lead your worst enemy to the saving knowledge of Jesus Christ? Who knows but that God will bring them to you, and you will get to lead them into the wonderful experience of salvation? When you stand on yonder shore, they could be there by His grace and love, and also because of your willingness to let Christ's love flow through you. I can think of no greater victory than to walk with my former enemy inside those pearly gates, both of us redeemed by the love of Jesus Christ.

"Then Jesus went about all the cities and villages, teaching in their synagogues, preaching the gospel of the kingdom, and healing every sickness and every disease among the people. But when He saw the multitudes, He was moved with compassion for them, because they were weary and scattered, like sheep having no shepherd." (Matthew 9:35-36) Notice what Jesus said next. *"And when He had called His twelve disciples to Him, He gave them power over unclean spirits, to cast them out, and to heal all kinds of sickness and all kinds of disease"* (Matthew 10:1). While compassion is the inevitable result of godly sorrow, the inevitable result of godly compassion is commitment. When Jesus saw the multitude he was moved with compassion

which moved him to commitment. He saw the great need of the multitude and committed the resources of his entire ministry to meeting the need.

Many times what we see moves us to anger, frustration, depression or fear instead of compassion. I have a hard time watching a news report about children who have been abused. I want to lash out at the abuser. Yet in my heart I know that nobody really wants to hurt a child. It's the devil working in them that causes them to be so cruel. The same devil that one time had you and me now has them. But for the grace of God we could be abusive. When Jesus saw people hurting He knew what was happening. Everyone who lashes out at children is hurting inside. Anyone who is abusive to his wife does so because of problems he has inside. When Jesus saw these people He was not moved with anger. He was moved with compassion, which moved Him to commitment.

When I was a pastor in New Orleans, early one morning I was on my way to the newspaper office to place an advertisement for our church. I was rushing down the sidewalk when all at once a drunk, who was coming down from the second story of a building, staggered out and bumped into me. He frightened me so I reacted by grabbing him by the collar. "You filthy drunk, watch where you are going!" I said. I straightened my suit and walked on down the sidewalk. Suddenly God spoke to me as clearly as could be and said, "Watch how you treat him. I gave my Son for him." My heart sank. I turned around and went back to the man who was still leaning against the wall right where I had shoved him. I said, "Sir, I'm so sorry for what I just did. You frightened me when you bumped me like that, but I should not have shoved you. Will you forgive me?" I asked if he had eaten breakfast yet. He told me he had not, so we went across the street to a restaurant where I ordered for him a hearty breakfast. When the meal was served, I prayed a blessing over it and over him. I paid his breakfast bill and went on my way.

That taught me a lesson. We can be so caught up in what we are doing that we forget to be considerate of what is happening to others. Very few people want to become a drunkard. We hold the key that can set them free. The church is the only one that can liberate them through the name of Jesus Christ.

Compassion, the greatest force known to mankind, moves you to act in a way that is pleasing to the Lord. Jesus saw the multitude and was moved with compassion. It moves you to action. Compassion moves you into the arena with another person and says, "I'm here to walk this out with you." I have seen many things accomplished during more than six decades of ministry. My desire is to finish the race exemplifying compassion in every part of my life.

During my pastorate in New Orleans an evangelist came to preach for us one weekend. He was staying at a historic, well-known hotel in the city. I parked my car in a parking garage just off of Canal Street one evening after services, ate with him and walked him back to his room. When I came back to my car, I paid the parking attendant so he would bring my car down. As I waited there an eleven or twelve-year old boy rode up on his bike. "Mr. Gorman!" he called out to me.

"Do I know you? How do I know you?" I asked him.

"See that store over there?" he pointed across the street. "Each day I go in there and watch you on television. I know who you are!"

I was amazed. I said, "Son, why are you out here at 1:30 a.m.?"

He shrugged, "Oh, I live here."

"What do you mean you live here? Where is your mother? Where is your daddy?"

"I don't know," he answered. "My mother and her boyfriend moved one day while I was gone. I don't know where they went."

I was deeply troubled. "Where do you sleep?" I asked him.

He pointed to a nearby furniture store and told me they put out big boxes in the alley each night for the trash pick-up. "I sleep in one of those boxes," he told me.

By this time my eyes were filled with tears. "Where do you eat?"

"Oh the restaurants around here give me food."

By that time, I was crying. I knelt down, hugged him, and emptied my pockets of the eight or ten dollars I had on me. I rolled up the bills and put them in his shirt pocket. The attendant drove up in my car as the young boy rode away on his bicycle. I drove away weeping. I could just picture one of my children in the same situation.

I finally cried out, "God this isn't right! I cannot change the situation of every child, but I can change some. If you will help me, I will give hope to every little child I can." I made a commitment to God, and I made a commitment to myself. That's how Teen Challenge came to Louisiana. Our church underwrote the whole thing because my heart went out to a little boy on the street. Today there are men in ministry who came through Teen Challenge of Louisiana. Because I was moved with compassion, I made a commitment to act. We had no money to do it. In fact, some of my board members thought I was nuts, but I was moved with compassion. Compassion doesn't stop and try to think of all the reasons it shouldn't act. Compassion sees the need, moves out, and causes something to happen to alleviate and correct the problem.

Today's church needs more compassion. We could fast twenty-one days, yet still not have compassion. Compassion is birthed in us by the power of the Holy Spirit and makes us quit thinking about ourselves. Compassion makes us deny ourselves and say, "We have to do this to help another."

When Hurricane Katrina hit New Orleans, one man was able to save the lives of forty-five people. A pastor friend of mine told him he was a hero. The man rejected this title and said, "My buddy got out seventy-seven people." The pastor replied, "Then both of you are heroes." The man shook his head and said, "No, you don't understand. My buddy got bit by a copperhead snake. He died. He's the real hero." His buddy wasn't thinking about the potential danger to himself; instead, he was thinking about saving lives.

There is a world all around drowning in sin, drugs and horrible things. We need to risk our lives to rescue them and bring them out. What would happen if we forgot about what people thought? I went into a bar one night to get a man out. People told me I should not have done that because somebody might have seen me and concluded that I had been drinking. Lots of people saw me on television in those days. Many church members were super-conscious of what I did. I told them that was their problem. My problem was to help that drunkard. If not for the grace of God we would all have been divorced or lying in a gutter or strung out on drugs. Christ gave himself for every person. Shall we do any less?

As Christians we have an awesome power through the Holy Spirit. We need to use it to alleviate the suffering of humanity. Without real compassion we won't do it. Compassion moves us to be concerned about people who walk into the church and the people who walk around outside of the church. I continually ask God to give the church the kind of compassion that causes us to make and fulfill our commitments. Then nothing can stop us from reaching out to the lost and hurting.

Compassion moves you to commitment. Compassion moves you to look beyond the fault to see the need. Compassion doesn't point a finger. When God wanted to reach a world that had totally rejected him, He loved us so much that He gave His only son. Jesus was filled with such compassion that no matter what was done to Him He kept on loving and fulfilling the mission for which He was sent. Before you were born again you didn't want Jesus, but He came to you anyway. When you weren't searching for Jesus, He was searching for you. What amazing compassion!

In New Orleans there is every kind of sin one can think of. When I served as a pastor there, the thought struck me that if the worst of all sinners in New Orleans got saved, no one else would have an excuse for not being saved. If the worst sickness was healed, every sick person could strive to believe God for their healing. I started praying, "God, send the worst sinner in this city to my church." God replied, "You're not ready for the worst sinner." I didn't like what He said, and I had no idea He was about to prove it to me.

One Sunday morning our church was almost full when suddenly the doors swung open. A woman walked in wearing a waitress' uniform. She walked up front and sat on the second pew. Do you know why she walked all the way up there? The saints were all sitting on the back pews! I saw her wipe tears from her eyes as I preached. When I gave the invitation she was the first one to kneel at the altar. Several of us prayed with her as she was beautifully born into the Kingdom. After she left the sanctuary, one of our church members walked up and said to me, "That's the meanest woman I have ever known. I live in her neighborhood. I can hear her cursing her children all the time. Why, she even whips her husband!" Later, I thanked the Lord for sending that woman to be saved.

I didn't know the test was really going to be that night. The song service was in full swing when the same lady walked in and started up to the front. I watched the doors open again, and in walked a girl in hot, hot, hot pants! She started walking toward the front of the sanctuary. I was shocked! I grabbed the phone which I kept on a little stand next to my chair on the platform and called my head usher. I told him to catch that woman with the hot pants and get her out of there. My usher told me he couldn't possibly get to her in time. Then he meekly asked, "Pastor, what am I going to do with her after I catch her?" That made me mad.

She sat on the second row right by the waitress who had just gotten saved that morning. I called the usher and told him to get his wife and some other board members' wives to go to the store the next day to get robes to put on these half-dressed women. The next day they purchased those robes, but we never used them. That same night after I preached she was the first person to kneel at the altar. I was glad she was at the altar, but I was worried about those hot pants and what people were going to say. I knew the "holier-than-thou" folks would be on the phone with me the next day. The little waitress who had been saved that morning was the only one kneeling beside her. Finally, a lady in our church knelt to pray with her leading her to Jesus Christ. She was gloriously saved. I had come down from the platform and was praying with others when I had the thought, "She is so happy she is going to hug everything in sight!" I knew the saints would feel she was going to contaminate their holy pastor if she hugged me, so I hurried to get up on the platform, but she caught me in a vigorous bear hug. I broke away while she shouted, "Hot dog, man! This is the best thing I ever found!"

When she turned to walk away, I could see what my church members had been staring at while she was hugging me. Her blue, hot pants had a pink heart on the back of them. Later, I was telling God how much I appreciated what He had done by saving those women. He said, "I told you that you weren't ready to see the worst sinner in New Orleans saved!" I realized then my compassion was too little. From that time on, I began to pray that I would be bathed in compassion.

The church today must cry out to be bathed in compassion because only then will it inspire us to action. Compassion exists because those who have sorrowed for their sins recognize how wonderful it is to be saved. They are eager to see others enjoy this same grace. Godly sorrow works repentance unto salvation, and godly compassion moves us to commit to action. Oh, how we need the blessing of sorrow, and the blessing of compassion working in our hearts today!

The pathway to inner healing is possible, but it can be dangerous as well. The danger is that those seeking inner healing may become overly focused on themselves. They may forget that there are others who are hurting too. The solution is to ask the Lord to give you true sorrow for your sins and true compassion for others. Out of this double blessing will come a life lived wonderfully and fully for the Lord Jesus Christ.

Peter sorrowed, repented, received the grace of God and spent the rest of his life compassionately sharing that blessing with others. The blessing of godly sorrow and the beautiful compassion it works in our hearts is necessary for us to bring in the harvest of souls for our Lord.

CHAPTER FOUR:
HEART PEACE

What disturbs your peace? It constantly amazes me how many people lack self-awareness. They cannot understand their own patterns of thinking. They have an overall sense of being disturbed, but are unaware of what is causing the disturbance. Counseling may be necessary for some; however, others can learn to develop a sense of self-awareness and learn to critically identify the things that disturb their peace.

Do you know that the Lord Jesus came to be our peace? He is Wonderful, Counselor and Prince of Peace. When we have that unsettled feeling, that twisting in our gut that something is wrong, we can use the blessing of repentance to begin the process of identifying the disturbance. We can go to Our Father and confess to Him that our peace is being disturbed. Perhaps we are not sleeping well. Perhaps we are feeling anxious and fearful. Sometimes we feel weighted down with cares and concerns. This is not living in the peace of God which Jesus won for us on the cross.

You might pray, "Oh God, I do not feel well. My peace is disturbed. I do not have the sense of well-being that I should have as your child. I confess this to you and repent. I would like to have you cleanse me of everything that disturbs my peace. Show me what has come between me and you."

If you will earnestly seek the Lord for what disturbs your peace, and if you will quietly listen for His response, He will teach you. He may speak a name to your heart. Suddenly you realize you have an issue with that person. Immediately ask for forgiveness. We are encouraged in scripture to live at peace with others. Perhaps the Lord will show you that you have spoken harshly to someone. Confess that to the Lord and ask to be cleansed. You may even need to go and ask that person to forgive you for your harsh words. I can never go to the pulpit and preach if I have spoken harshly or carelessly to my wife. I just can't do it. I have to go to her and say, "Honey, please forgive me. I'll try to do better."

Before Virginia and I were married, I hardly had time to court. I was the pastor of a church, worked a full-time job in town and preached revivals. Most of our dates were while driving to a revival service. One night we were driving to a meeting. While I was thinking about the message for the night, Virginia was talking ninety miles an hour. I was trying to meditate and pray. After a while, I turned to her and said, "Would you please shut up?" I was so preoccupied that it came out of my mouth before I knew it. I have apologized for that one million and one times and I can assure you that never happened again! See, the Lord is the author of peace. He wants peace between you and others.

The Apostle Paul said, *"If it is possible, as much as depends on you, live peaceably with all men"* (Romans 12:18). Paul was a leader in the church. He recognized that it was not always possible, but he shouldered his responsibility for peace. Some people will not be at peace with you; however, you can choose whether or not you will be at peace with them. Your

Wonderful Counselor, your Prince of Peace can prompt your heart during prayer showing you what disturbs your peace.

What does peace mean? Jesus said, "My peace I give." His peace is serenity, quiet, secure and undisturbed. If that is what it means, then you must arrive at a place where you have peace that does not depend on what someone else does or doesn't do. You must let the peace of God rule and reign. This peace is dependent on what Christ has done, not what someone else may or may not do. You can have peace come hell or high water. Perhaps there are storms all around you, but God is in control. Fear and peace cannot abide in your heart at the same time. You cannot have peace and hatred at the same time. Peace and bitterness cannot exist in you at the same time. The scriptures teach us that we must strive for peace. This means effort is required on our part. We must not wait until the other party decides to be at peace. We must make the decision to be at peace in spite of what they decide to do.

The Psalmist David said, *"Depart from evil and do good; seek peace and pursue it"* (Psalm 34:14). Jesus wept over Jerusalem saying, *"If you had known, even you, especially in this your day, the things that make for your peace! But now they are hidden from your eyes"* (Luke 19:42). You can know, in this your day, the things that make for peace if you will just go to Jesus and inquire of Him. David encouraged us to put some muscle to it. Seek. Pursue. Drive hard toward peace.

True heart peace is the absence of guilt. Is it really possible to live without guilt? Absolutely! If we choose to live a lifestyle of repentance, we can live a life without the weighty bondage of guilt. "Lord, I repent of the guilt I feel." The instant I pray, the Holy Spirit will shine His light into my life to show me what is causing my guilt. When I confess and repent, Jesus can wash the guilt away and set my heart free with peace.

Once the Holy Spirit shows you what was disturbing your peace, you must make a conscious decision to stay out of that trap again. The enemy of our souls is not a creator. The devil just keeps trying the same things over and over again because they usually work. When you make a conscious decision to change, you can offer your life to the Holy Spirit for constant guidance and direction. It's like having regular check-ups.

When I bought a new car, I realized I would have to take it to the garage at different intervals for tune-ups and maintenance. Did I have to do this because I was a horrible driver? No! I did this because I realized I live in a dirty world with all sorts of pollutants that can impair my car's operating condition. Although I know very little about computers, I do know that every so often it is wisdom to run a systems check for viruses. I know that as time passes the everyday use can cause my computer to be potentially exposed to viruses. It is a wise person who takes the time to do regular check-ups on his own soul. We must make a firm decision to avoid at all costs those things that once disturbed our peace, and if they are found in us again, we must promptly deal with them by repentance.

After you have regained your peace by confession and repentance, you must regain authority over your own life. Realize that your peace does not depend on what others do or do not do for you. Realize that true heart peace comes from a right and healthy relationship with your Heavenly Father through Jesus Christ. If you find yourself avoiding fellowship and devotions with the Lord, ask yourself: what has disturbed my peace?

Relationships work both ways. If I profess I love and cherish my children and grandchildren, but never bother to call and talk with them, how much do I truly love them? Relationships require time and attention. If you say you have a relationship with your Heavenly Father, be willing to spend time speaking to Him and listening to Him. You have the right and the responsibility to use your spiritual vigor to accomplish this. Anything worthwhile takes effort. It is superabundantly worthwhile to have fellowship with your Heavenly Father.

Retaking authority over your own life is the same as retaking control and accepting responsibility for the condition of your own heart and mind. Christ Jesus has won for us this authority. You have as much authority as you have the power to back it up. I could tell you that a bar of gold was yours, but if that bar was so heavy that you could not move it, it would be of very little value to you. You would have the authority to take it, but without the strength and power to move it, your authority would be useless. Many Christians do not exercise the authority God has given them because they have never recognized the power which stands behind it.

The power of the Spirit of God who raised Jesus from the dead dwells in every Spirit-filled believer. How powerful was that Spirit who raised Jesus from the dead? The Holy

Spirit is so powerful He not only raised Jesus from the dead, but He also lifted Christ above all principalities and powers and seated Him at the right hand of God the Father. *"For by Him all things were created that are in heaven and that are on earth, visible and invisible, whether thrones or dominions or principalities or powers. All things were created through Him and for Him"* (Colossians 1.16). When Jesus Christ came forth from the dead, He declared, *"All power is given unto Me in heaven and in earth"* (Matthew 28.18, KJV). The Greek word which is translated "power" in this verse also has the meaning "authority." Now, His authority works in us by His Holy Spirit.

His strength works in us by our conscious dependence on Jesus Christ. How interesting that strength is dependent! Many people think their strength makes them independent, but that thought becomes their downfall. Our strength is dependent upon our surrendering to the Lord.

A good example of this kind of dependency upon Christ is found in a message preached by the Apostle Paul. Paul was a powerful man, greatly used of God so much so that demons came out when Paul spoke. One day a demonized young woman was following Paul so he turned to her and spoke, "In the name of Jesus," and the demon immediately left her. On another occasion when Paul saw a severely crippled man, he said, "Stand upright on your feet." Immediately the man was healed. Each time Paul manifested a conscious dependence on the person of Jesus Christ, which caused him to exercise the authority and spiritual vigor necessary to see lives changed. Your spiritual strength is directly related to your conscious dependence on Jesus Christ.

A person's peace is often disturbed by the poison of a Pharisaical spirit. Possibly the most devastating thing that can happen to any believer is to be so blind that the Pharisaical spirit operates undetected in his life. It is a Pharisaical spirit that makes one feel that what he is doing in the name of righteousness, justifies the means he uses to accomplish it. Jesus called it straining at a gnat, but swallowing a camel.

A good example of the Pharisaical spirit at work is found in the case of a young man who murdered an abortion doctor. How was his murder any different than the murders taking place inside the abortion clinics? I hate abortion, but I am not for the protests that often create a hostile atmosphere. The news cameras love to play on this and try to catch professing Christians acting in a most un-Christ-like manner.

Jesus warned of the leaven of the Pharisees. He concluded that a little leaven will spoil the whole lump of dough. The moment you get to the point you feel that you have arrived, you become self-righteous. At that moment you cannot admit you have a problem. Self-righteousness keeps us from realizing that our sin is as great as the next man's sin. This disturbs our peace with God.

One time I had the opportunity to minister to a prisoner whose wife attended our church. He was a great, big guy who stood about 6' 5" and weighed about 250 pounds. He got saved and received the Holy Spirit. He enrolled in Bible correspondence studies and was making top scores on every test. I ministered to him frequently. Then one day I made the mistake of asking his wife why he was in prison. She dropped her head and was silent. I said, "You don't have to talk about it if you don't want to." Then she finally answered, "Yes, I feel you should know. When he was drunk and on drugs, he stomped our five-year old son to death." I was stunned, but then I had to ask myself a question. If I had known that before he was saved, would I have been able to accept him? His wife continued, "That is why I come to the altar every service because I have difficulty forgiving him." I had to go home and repent. I realized my sin of a vengeful attitude was the same as his sin of murdering his own son. Self-righteousness keeps us from seeing our own sin while pointing out another's. There can be no peace with God while a Pharisaical spirit dwells in us.

As God begins to change us, He always starts in our heart and then works outwardly. He never tries to change us on the outside before He has cleaned up the inside. He works with us on things that disturb our peace. He wants us to be at peace with Him, with others and within our own heart.

In almost every city you can find churches where they will tell you what you should do from the time you get up in the morning until you go to bed at night. These Pharisees pride themselves on being holier than anybody else. They are so busy telling you what to do and what not to do that they miss the true way to holiness. They shine up the outside every day and make it look holy. They set all kinds of rules and regulations to abide by in order to be holly. Dresses are a certain length, hair is a certain length, face is a certain color or no color at all, and sleeves are a certain length. Too often, they have an outward form of godliness, but no inward holiness. Jesus was pretty straight- forward with people like this. *"Woe to you, scribes and Pharisees, hypocrites! For you are like whitewashed tombs which indeed appear beautiful outwardly, but inside are full of dead men's bones and all uncleanness"* (Matthew 23:27).

One of these people visited our church one day. He confronted me after service, "Your wife is not very modest."

I replied, "What do you mean?"

He said, "When she walked across the platform during the service, I saw her knees."

"You vulgar thing, what were you doing looking at my wife's knees?" I reprimanded. Here he was trying to act so holy by confronting me about my wife's clothing, when he was the one with the problem. People like this run around trying to make everyone else appear holy on the outside. You can't make people holy from the outside.

Pharisee spirits disturb our peace with God. Pharisees love to make judgments. We have to stop letting things provoke us into making judgments. When we become judgmental, we have sealed ourselves off from being wrong in our own eyes. If we admit to ourselves we are wrong in some areas, we should not judge others. Sadly, in order to preserve our "right" to judge, we choose to ignore areas in which we are wrong. Often judgmental people are also gossips who love to talk and pass judgments against others.

The Pharisaical spirit loves to evaluate and reveal how others do not measure up, but he almost always has an ulterior motive. For instance, if I judge a man, then I may be afraid a person over here might find out I was wrong, so I have to sell him on the idea of this other man's guilt. I have to convince him the other man is no-good because I certainly don't want him to discover my faults and failures. Now I've done serious damage to the body of Christ. Hypocrisy is a deadly poison that destroys the body of Christ. The only antidote is sincere repentance.

A thorough search of the scriptures will reveal the Pharisaical spirit has three powerful weapons in its arsenal. Manipulation, domination and control are deadly and damning in the hands of those controlled by this destructive spirit. I served as pastor at one church where there were about five wives whose husbands didn't come to church very often, but then their husbands got saved. The wives would never forgive their husbands for their past sins. It angered each woman that her husband had come to Christ because it showed he was not as mean and horrible as she had declared him to be.

Anybody who puts down their mate to someone else is trying to cover up something wrong in their own life. They are trying to hide something. I'm not referring to speaking privately with a counselor or minister in order to sincerely search for help. I'm talking about a companion who says in the company of others, "I don't know why I ever married my spouse!" Perhaps that person is trying to hide their own ignorance or faults. Whenever a spouse gets saved and begins to walk in their salvation experience, they may go through hell at home because their new-found humility is going to show up their mate's hypocrisy. Some wives don't really want their husbands to change because they get a lot of mileage out of being the "tragic heroine" in their little dramas.

They have learned a little trick called manipulation. As long as I can make you feel that you are fortunate that I'd even speak to you, I can keep you as my emotional servant. Some never get out from under that sort of manipulation. They are filled with anger. Have you ever seen somebody go around like a little puppy? You may say, "That's probably the meekest person I've ever seen." However, sometimes they have more hidden anger per square inch than any other human being living. They know that if they get out of line they will catch wrath. So they act meek and mild when all the time they are boiling inside. When you do something out of fear it makes you angry because you're being manipulated.

I know my wife teasingly manipulates me at times, and I respond gladly. I'm not going to leave that honey bowl! Let her just keep filling it up. But, I'm not really being manipulated. I'm jumping in with both feet. There's a difference between being dragged in and jumping in. There has to be a little of that in every marriage. That's not what I'm talking about. What I am talking about is when your mate manipulates you into doing something and all the time you resent it. You are angry. You feel worthless. When that is going on, then you are being manipulated. Your peace is being disturbed.

Manipulation will disarm you to the point you feel so worthless that, if you lose that certain person, you think you cannot survive. That is why so many wives stay in abusive relationships. Manipulation has them under lock and key. God has not designed the marriage relationship to include manipulation. Manipulation is a nasty weapon.

Another powerful weapon is domination. Domination disturbs the peace of everyone living in the household. I was counseling a man when I finally had to tell him, "There's not a thing in the world wrong except that you have just cowed down to your wife until she is lording it over you, but you will not stand up."

He protested, "You just don't know! If I stand up to her, she will leave me."

I wasn't very accommodating. "First of all, where would she go? Secondly, what would be better? Should she stay and you remain miserable and destroyed or will you stand up and be a man and see what happens?" I counseled with him several weeks concerning the matter of domination. One day she was on a rampage putting him down and telling him all sorts of things which made him feel demoralized. Suddenly, the husband stood up and said, "Be quiet now. I'm not having any more of this. You have dogged me long enough. The game is over." The wife was stunned into silence.

Sometime later, she mentioned to me how proud she was of her husband, and how she was learning to be the wife she always wanted to be. "I felt I had to be so strong because I always thought he was too weak," she explained. "When he stood up to me that day I realized he meant it and I would have to give up the driver's seat. I have and he is driving just fine without me telling him his every move." This couple is still married today. They enjoy a strong respect for each other. The wife learned domination was no longer permitted. She repented of her domineering ways and the fear which drove her to cling so tightly to the steering wheel. Her husband took authority over his own life, and took responsibility for what was disturbing his peace. He set his house in order. Domination had to go. Mutual love and respect rule in their home today.

Control is the third powerful weapon of the Pharisaical spirit. Control can be demonstrated emotionally, physically and spiritually. Controllers are not content with having an opinion. They must require everyone else to agree with their opinion. Controllers are eager to cast stones and bring down judgments. Outwardly, they appear powerful and self-confident, but inwardly they are wracked with fear. Their fear is that others will learn about their deficiencies. In order to cover them, controllers are driven to control others.

One man controlled every penny his wife spent. He constantly tongue lashed her about spending. Outwardly, he appeared to be powerful and in control when secretly his own financial decisions had reduced the family to nothing. He knew that his wife was a better money manager. Instead of turning over the family finances to her and humbling himself to be taught, he was continually over-drafting the accounts. Then he would race to cover his weakness by launching a verbal tirade at her when she brought home the family groceries. He was a controller who was controlled by the Pharisaical spirit.

Some of you are, no doubt, controlled by your children. You never pray for the pastor of the church. You never pray for the sick or injured because every prayer is saturated with cries to God for your rebellious children. Sure, God wants you to make your requests known, but some of you have to cut the apron strings and let the child face the consequences of his own behavior. Your child controls you so completely that you would never talk to Jesus if it weren't for Junior's frequent mistakes.

Some people use put-downs and sarcasm to control others. It makes them feel exalted to push others down. People can be controlled by certain emotional reactions from others. How many have felt manipulated or controlled by the tears of another?

I learned early on in my childhood that emotional control was just not going to work on my mother. If I misbehaved she would promise to thrash me with the peach tree switch. Sometimes she would delay the punishment, and I would get as sweet as sugar. I would be so helpful around the house thinking that she would soon have occasion to forget her promise. If my daddy threatened me with punishment and then delayed it, I would rejoice for I knew I was off the hook. It wasn't long before he would just forget, but my mother never forgot anything. At the end of the day, she would tell me to go cut her a switch. I knew that no amount of whining or crying was going to deliver me from the spanking. In fact, if I tried to work that emotional manipulation or control over her, I would get spanked even harder. I learned my mother would not be controlled.

Some Christians are so controlled by another's anger to such a degree they cannot make their own decisions. They constantly second guess themselves. They feel inadequate, dumb and incapable. The wife can't decide if she should buy wheat bread or white bread for fear her husband's anger will flare against her. Some parents won't deny their children anything for fear their anger will flare and the children will throw temper tantrums. My children learned early on that neither their mother nor their father would be controlled by their emotional outbursts. I've heard mothers tell their little ones they can't have a candy bar, but by the time they get through the check-out line, they have the chocolate half eaten. Her Junior was able to control his mother by the threat of his emotional outburst. That mistake today is costing her about a dollar, but what will it cost her when Junior is demanding a new car?

Anger can be used to control, but anger has no place in the life of a Christian. Some pastors are controlled by members of their flock and refuse to bring correction to ungodly behavior. They worry that if they bring Biblical correction, the church member will flare up in anger and lash out at the pastor. They fear the retribution the angry member may dish out. The problem is that the anger should not exist in the heart of the member in the first place.

Some pastors are controlled by money. They worry that godly correction will cause a member to withdraw from the church and take his tithes check with him. I say, "Let him go!

If you do not want to be molded and shaped by the Word of God, take your money and go." God will bring in folks who do want to be molded and shaped by God. In all probability the newcomers will be more generous to the coffers of the church than the angry member who just stalked out.

Perhaps the thing that controls church members more than anything else is what one pastor friend calls the "odorless, tasteless, carbon monoxide called pride." Pride is what fuels the Pharisee. Pharisees are usually Pharisees because they cannot clearly see. They are the ones who mock a young woman for having hips that are too plump and can't see that their own nose is too big. Pride picks at others, yet seems remarkably incapable of seeing itself.

Christians often have their peace disturbed by the prideful actions of others. Unfortunately, often the most detrimental thing in a Christian's life is his own undiagnosed pride. Jesus did not warn us about the Pharisees. He warned us about the leaven of the Pharisees. What was He saying? Just as leaven or yeast is the operating force that makes dough rise in the bread, pride makes the spirit of the Pharisee rise in us.

As a child, I remember watching my mother make bread. The yeast would cause that flat blob of dough to rise until the whole house would smell fragrant and yeasty. Sometimes she got too busy to get it into the oven in time so she would have to punch it down and let it rise again. If that leaven of the Pharisees rises in you, the Holy Spirit may come and punch you down and let you start all over again. It happened to me.

In 1978 I made a tragic mistake. I turned my back on principles that had been the guiding force of my life. I committed an act of adultery. A minister's wife, whom I was counseling at the time, called my office and led me to believe that her emotional situation was so desperate she was contemplating suicide. I foolishly abandoned my ministerial protocol and hurriedly went by myself to her hotel room. My transgression became a dark, ominous cloud hanging over my life and ministry. During the months and years that followed, I repented daily to the Lord, but kept the transgression hidden in my heart. A heavy haze of fear hovered over me like a menacing giant although the church I pastored in New Orleans had grown from 100 members to several thousand members. We had five services each Sunday, a Monday evening miracle rally, and two services each Wednesday. Our daily television ministry included a question and answer session with live callers from all across the United States. We were in the process of purchasing two television stations. A few years earlier I had been elected to the Executive Board of the Assemblies of God. I was at the apex of my ministry.

In July of 1986, the woman's husband confronted me about my transgression. He confronted me after being counseled to do so by an attorney, another pastor, an evangelist, one of his co-workers and his wife. One mighty hand punched the pride right out of my dough and exposed my sin.

The only remedy to pride is the raw and laborious scrubbing of the Holy Spirit on the inside of our hearts and minds. This scrubbing, which is so intensely painful, includes not only having to deal with our own failures, but having to see the terrible effects our failures have on others. I watched, broken and helpless, as my shattered wife and children felt the full effects of my transgression. I mourned for my family and my church family. I mourned for myself. I lay helplessly before the Lord, day after day, begging Him to give us the strength to survive. I was humbled and amazed that I had allowed this terrible act to affect so many lives. Unfounded lies and accusations were hurled toward me. I was defenseless because my own transgression had opened the door to accusations. The leaven of pride caused me to fear total destruction until the Spirit brought the truth to me that through repentance I could be restored.

It was a long time before my soul and spirit began to recover enough that I could minister to the Lord's people again. When I did, it was with a sweeter, softer and kinder spirit than the one I had previously possessed. I learned what it was like to fail, to fall to pride and to accept with humility my own actions and the consequences. That is why I like the quote that says, "The bird with the broken wing may never fly high, but oh how sweet is his new song!"

It is ironic that Elvis Presley made famous a song by Thomas Dorsey called, *There Will Be Peace in the Valley.* Elvis knew very little of that peace in his lifetime. Drugs and alcohol stole his peace. Other famous singers like Dolly Parton, Loretta Lynn and Johnny Cash have added their voices to this song which says, "There will be peace in the valley for me someday." Many ministers and fellow Christians appreciate the message of this song.

Peace in the valley for me someday? I say, "Why wait until someday comes? Why not enjoy this kind of peace today?" True heart peace is found at the feet of Jesus where all your sins and transgressions are washed and cleansed. Heart peace is found when you regularly come before the throne of God asking Him to show you what disturbs your peace. When you respond in true humility and repentance, peace will keep your heart and mind by Christ Jesus—this day, not someday. *"And God's peace [shall be yours, that tranquil state of a soul assured of its salvation through Christ, and so fearing nothing from God and being content with its earthly lot of whatever sort that is, that peace] which transcends all understanding shall garrison and mount guard over your hearts and minds in Christ Jesus* (Philippians 4:7, AMP).

CHAPTER FIVE:
PERFECT LOVE CASTS OUT FEAR

The Spirit of fear unleashed in the land is hounding God's people. Like a vicious dog, it preys on their emotions and freezes their spiritual walk. I have been in much prayer about this because so many of God's people are battling with fear, real fear. I went with a pastor recently to pray for the sick. When I returned to my office, there was a message from another pastor. I called him and he confided that he was almost paralyzed by fear. I am troubled in my spirit because fear is keeping so many Christians from receiving what God has for them.

The Apostle Paul took the time to address this subject with his spiritual son, Timothy, when he wrote, *"For God has not given us a spirit of fear, but of power and of love and of a sound mind"* (II Timothy 1:7). Why would Paul write such a thing? A lot of things were taking place in Timothy's life. He was doing battle because of Paul's imprisonment. Timothy was even afraid to go and visit his spiritual father. He was afraid of the authorities and afraid to be identified with Paul. Paul later said, *"Do not be ashamed of me that I am in prison."* Timothy was being tormented by the spirit of fear. Paul sent the truth of God's Word to arrest this tormenting spirit.

He spoke to Timothy saying, *"God has not given..."* God has not let you come to where you are in order to be defeated. Paul dislodged the thought from Timothy's mind that somehow God was the cause of his fear. God is not fear. God is love. Paul was saying, "Look, Timothy, God is in control here." He wanted him to see God had not opened the door for fear to come on Timothy. Timothy lived in a time when, to be identified with Jesus Christ, was to invite persecution. We have brothers and sisters living in other countries who suffer this same situation today. Nevertheless, God speaks to them by saying, "Look, I haven't caused that to come on you. That spirit of fear is not from me."

Someone might ask why the Lord even permits persecutions to come. Let me answer that question with a question. How are you going to rule and reign with Christ if you haven't even learned to rule your own spirit in times of crisis? We want to reign, but we don't want to go through the molding and shaping it takes to make us good rulers. Persecution has a way of doing that, so sometimes God permits it. He will not let you be carried around on a feather pillow. He wants you to learn to rule and reign even when trouble comes, even when fear tries to prevail. God wants us to learn how to stand in authority just like a good ruler has to learn to stand in authority and use his authority for the common good.

God wants us to understand our authority over fear. Does He cause fear? Absolutely not! God is not the author of evil. Every good and perfect gift comes down from Him. Evil does not come from God! Timothy was confused about the matter, so Paul took time to clear it up for him. It is true that Satan often comes in seeming so strong and makes it appear that you might be totally wiped out, but even if you fall down or are knocked down, God can help you up again. He has not caused the spirit of fear to come upon you. Paul wanted that important truth first and foremost in Timothy's mind.

Knowing what God has not given is important. Understanding what God has given us is absolutely essential. Perfect love casts out fear. Paul was teaching Timothy what it seems to take many Christians a lifetime to learn. The remedy for fear is love. If you love Jesus Christ perfectly and completely, and if you know beyond a shadow of a doubt He loves you perfectly and completely, that kind of love will smash into pieces the spirit of fear. The reason so many are still struggling with fear is they have not learned to love and be loved. Love is the strongest force in the whole world. Your enemy may try to destroy you and perhaps do a pretty good job, but if you choose the higher road of love, you will eventually have the victory. You may lose your house, your career and your health, but you won't lose the war if you choose to love.

Though the victory has already been won for us, we have to choose to enter into that victory by living like Jesus did. Fear is robbing Christian people. Fear dominates and faith takes a walk. The doctors once told me that my health was such that I would not be able to continue in the ministry. I knew that God loved me and had called me to this task. I knew that He would help me, so I continued in the ministry surviving many more years than the doctors thought. Because I was absolutely certain of my calling, worry had to flee.

Thoughts of worry often come like termites to eat up your house when you aren't really even aware of it. These thoughts start out with, "I wonder... I wonder what I will do if I lose my job. I wonder if my husband is going to leave me." Thoughts like this go on and on, and can cause us to not even realize we are being destroyed. Stop wondering. Start believing that the God who loves you and calls you His own is able to take care of you.

The truth is God will withhold no good thing from you. We have to remember this in the same context that Jesus did. God withheld no good thing from Jesus, but Jesus did not live the lifestyle of the typical American. God didn't promise to uphold some culture's idea of blessing. He promised to uphold His idea of blessing. Some people think that if they don't have a big screen television God doesn't love them. Others think if they are not driving a new car they aren't living in the blessing of God. God isn't required to bless you according to your cultural expectations. He promised to bless you according to His standards.

Fear makes you hold to wrong ideas about God and yourself. Fear aggravates and torments. Fear puts people into bondage, but God hasn't given us a spirit of fear. He has given us love.

One day after the public revelation of my sin, I sat in my den, nestling my beautiful baby granddaughter in my arms. As I ran my fingers through her soft hair, the reality of my situation gripped me with great intensity. I was almost paralyzed with the thought that one day she might have to unfairly bear the agonizing consequences of her grandfather's mistake. The pain I was living with became excruciating. My fears were well-founded. When the information was publicized, I did lose my home, my possessions, my church and my reputation. I know well the truth of the scripture, "Fear has torment."

I also learned the truth of that entire verse. *"There is no fear in love; but perfect love casts out fear, because fear involves torment. But he who fears has not been made perfect in love"* (I John 4:18). When I confessed, with great sorrow, my terrible sin to my wife, my children, the leaders of my church and my friends, I had to learn to rely on their love for me. It was like a healing balm. I had no right to expect my wife to forgive me and love me anyway, but she did. I received the greatest gift I could ever have in the form of her forgiveness, and her loyal devotion to me. That kind of love, perfect love, began to banish the fear that had tormented me for years.

When we truly understand that while we were yet sinners Christ died for us, we can understand His bountiful love. It is this blessed assurance of His great love that overcomes the fear. A missionary friend of mine was building a large Bible school in India. One day he had run out of money. His wife said to him, "Mark, isn't today the day we must pay $10,000? What will we do?"

My friend replied, "Honey, we don't need it until 2 p.m. today."

Later that morning he went to the post office where he discovered a check for $10,000. Human nature in us resists the thought of living day to day, but sometimes God lets us run down to the wire to prove a point, perhaps to us and perhaps to the devil.

The devil jumps on us and makes accusations against God. He tries to make us believe God is failing us. Fear and panic set in. Jesus addressed this so beautifully when He pointed to the field of lilies that day. "Look at these," He taught. "They do not need to lift a hand for their own provision, but they are so beautifully clothed by God Himself." He motioned to the sparrow flitting about. "Look how well My Father has provided for these," He said. Then He turned to the people and said, "Are you not worth much more than these?" Sure we are! If you aren't careful, however, you will sin by believing God loves the sparrows more than His children. The devil will jump on you and make you doubt God's love.

The devil thought if he stripped me of all my material possessions I would give up on God. He sorely underestimated my love. Something roared to life inside me, "I was called to preach! Hell is not going to stop me!" Love, my love for my Savior, lifted me. There is such power in love.

God has not given me the spirit of fear, but He has given me power. This power is so strong it can help me overcome every obstacle. I can defeat the devil, and rebuke the spirit of fear by this wonder-working power. Am I really more powerful than the devil? Absolutely, if I hold on to the promises of God! When the devil attacked me with sickness, I held on to the promises God had made to me concerning the ministry. I called on my promises until they became like a sword in my hand. I reminded the devil of what God had promised me and I confessed that I would see those promises come to pass. Some would have sat down in a rocking chair and waited to die, but I had some souls to see saved and some devils to chase off. I had to fight the good fight of faith. I had to lay hold of that which was laid up for me. It took effort and it took faith in God's abiding love for me. I pushed through those physical battles, and won because I had the power of my promises.

I also had the power of the Holy Spirit in my life. When you surrender your life to Jesus Christ and ask for the gift of the Holy Spirit, power comes into your life. You are not fighting a battle with a wet noodle, but with a sharp, two-edged sword. You are slicing away at the lies that Satan throws at you. You are powerful because the Holy Spirit within you is God Almighty doing battle on your behalf. God has not given me the spirit of fear, but of power. I am powerful, or full of power because of the Holy Spirit in me.

Paul reminded Timothy that God has also given us a sound mind. All too often it is a person's thinking that gets him into trouble. *"As a man thinks in his heart so is he..."* (Proverbs 23:7a). If you think you can't overcome, you probably will not. Some of you are waiting for someone to come in and lay hands on you and magically give you victory. You can be free when you learn to meditate on the Word of God. The Holy Scriptures are able to make you wise. They are well able to change your heart and mind. You have to decide to meditate and then you have to practice it. There are no shortcuts here. You have to dwell on God's Word. Roll it over and over in your mind and let it cast down arguments and accusations which your uncontrolled mind might make against God.

"Well, I just don't feel God is for me!" someone whines. The Word says, "If God is for me who can be against me!" You have to decide what you will choose to think about. Change your thinking and you will change the way you act.

One night I was in spiritual warfare. Suddenly, a voice spoke into my ear, "If God is for us who can be against us?" I got out of bed and began praising God, speaking in tongues and glorifying Him. The peace and joy of the Lord flooded my soul. We can be victorious if we get our thought life right.

We need to stop walking around acting like we are defeated. We belong to the King of Kings. We can walk around victorious because He said so. That doesn't mean walk around in arrogance and hostility, but with quiet confidence. Why? Because we know in whom we have believed and are persuaded He will keep that which we have committed to Him.

Can you tell when a lady is feeling good about herself--for instance, when she leaves the beauty salon with her hair styled and her nails freshly done? She is wearing a beautiful dress. She just glows with confidence because she knows she is beautiful. She is grinning like a possum eating persimmons! She feels beautiful, so she acts beautiful.

You take that same woman and let fear pounce on her and the whole picture falls apart. The devil starts whispering about the run in her hose or whether her dress makes her look fat. Pretty soon her shoulders are slumping and she is just slinking out of the room hoping no one sees her. What happened? She listened to the wrong voice. She let the wrong thought get control of her mind. You watch that same lady when she walks in beauty with quiet confidence, singing the praises of God, unwilling for her peace to be destroyed. The devil walks on by saying, "Nope, I can't do anything with that one!"

The devil knows most church-going, Christian people aren't going to go gamble away their money at the casino. He starts with something he thinks he can use to cause them to stumble. He starts with fear. Then he tries to get that entrenched into a person's mind. The devil is able to stop so many people with fear. Unfortunately, fear transfers. If you put one fearful person in the room, pretty soon the whole room is swept up in fear. You have to keep the door shut with the power of the Word of God by the Holy Spirit. The devil can't pick a Holy Ghost lock!

If that same lady keeps singing the praises of God and glorifying Jesus Christ, the devil can't find a place to operate. He has to go on down the road. Meditate on the Word of God and that will change your way of thinking. You will begin to say, "Others may not love me, but I know my Heavenly Father is just crazy about me." You'll begin to believe that and it will change your way of thinking. God hasn't given you a spirit of fear, but He has given you a sound mind.

Fear is one of the main tools Satan uses to keep us from being all God wants us to be. Every place I go, I deal with people who are in bondage to fear. It is time we get it scripturally correct regarding fear and how to get victory over it. In the Book of Job, we read that Job lamented, *"For the thing I greatly feared has come upon me, and what I dreaded has happened to me"* (Job 3:25). When Satan began to destroy Job's possessions, Job immediately began to fear for his children. In the following verse he said that he had not even made it to safety nor had he a moment's rest before the tragic news came to him. "Yet trouble came," Job said. People don't realize what happens when they open the door to fear. It is like an invitation for other devils to attack. The next thing you know the devil has launched many fearful thoughts into your mind. If you accept them and start speaking them out or acting on them, an onslaught of hell is heading your way.

I remember the first time a Spirit of intercession came upon me. True intercession is when the Holy Spirit takes over with such dynamics and force you literally are not in control. This happened to me as a sixteen-year-old boy. I began interceding about a revival I was going to preach. Intercession came on me and for forty-five minutes I was in a fetal position with travail and groaning. Suddenly something broke in the spiritual realm. Following this experience, a spirit of fear attacked me in an effort to prevent me from ever allowing the Spirit to use me in that manner again. Fear came on me with questions about if I did this again what would happen to me spiritually, physically and emotionally. The devil tried to make me believe I would lose total control of my mind and emotions. Satan keeps people from doing what God wants by attacking with the spirit of fear.

Job was an amazing person. I know this because when God singles you out and starts talking about how holy and righteous you are; you must be on the top of His list. Still Job admitted that he was attacked by fear. Satan comes to many and begins to torment them by saying what God has given is going to be taken away. Mothers fear their children will die suddenly. Fathers fear they will be afflicted and not be able to provide for their families. Fear is a spirit that can readily transfer from person to person if they are not living in the love of Jesus Christ. Gideon's army had to be shaved down to a bare minimum because God told Gideon to send the fearful home. God didn't want those given over to the spirit of fear to contaminate the others. Fear destroys armies, countries, marriages, homes and families. People begin to act according to what they fear or what they believe and suddenly their whole world starts to fall apart.

Some books and preachers will tell you if you go through troubles and trials something is wrong with your faith. In Job's case, something was right with his faith. Paul suffered many devastating losses. What was wrong with his faith? Nothing! In fact the trial came to him because his faith was being perfected.

Some people complain against God saying, "God gave it to me, so why did He let me lose it?" Sometimes God allows loss because He wants us to take inventory of our lives. Yes, in this life we will suffer tribulation, but we can be of good cheer for our Lord and Savior has overcome this world and all its sorrows. We may not understand why loss comes our way, but if we push through and remain faithful to God we will understand it all by and by. When Hurricane Katrina hit New Orleans in 2005, I did not understand why my house was destroyed. God had given me that house, yet in one day it was ruined.

I prayed and sought God. I poured my heart out to Him. I searched for understanding. I said, "Lord you gave me that house." We had suffered false accusations and even bankruptcy. God spoke to a man from Ohio whom I had only met twice. He had graciously provided the financing for me to purchase a house even though I was in the midst of bankruptcy. Then the hurricane came and in one day the house was ruined. Did God give it to me or not? I searched my heart listening for the answer. Finally, I understood. Did I serve God or did I serve that house? If I never got an answer would I still keep serving Him? I refused to let perishable things control me.

People came to us and told us the government would take care of us. They wanted to loan us a very small FEMA (Federal Emergency Management Agency) trailer. Instead, God opened a door for us to move from Louisiana to Missouri. We could hold on to perishable things, blame God and damage our relationship with the Lord, or we could accept the storm and its consequences and move on. God gave us the strength to move on. I was retirement age. I could have just sat down and accepted this as defeat. I did not. I moved on and continued to do the work of God.

Families today are in bondage because of insecurities they feel about their finances. They haven't learned to let God take care of them. I already knew something about letting God take care of us. In 1986 my retirement, life insurance and health insurance benefits were stripped away. On top of that, in 1995 I had a heart attack. Have you ever tried to get life insurance after a heart attack? It was almost impossible.

Letters came from Christians. Some of them called me a failure and turned their backs on me. They recommended I quit the ministry. I didn't accept their counsel. I know the gifts and callings of God are without repentance. He didn't change His mind about me just because I failed Him.

If trials and tribulations are an indication you have missed God, then Paul must have missed God by a mile. He must have lived his entire life out of the will of God. He was shipwrecked, snake bit, beaten, thrown out for dead, homeless, cold, hungry, in prison, you name it. Paul had his plate full of tribulations. Nevertheless, we now regard him as the greatest Christian example outside of Jesus Christ. He used his trials to draw on the comfort of the Holy Spirit, then turned and offered that same comfort to others who suffered trials as well.

If everything falls easily into your hands and you never endure hardship, how will you encourage others who are less fortunate? It is during times like these, this scripture is made real to us, *"You are of God, little children, and have overcome them, because He who is in you is greater than he who is in the world"* (I John 4:4). You can chant that all day long, but rest assured your life may have to prove it. Choose to have confidence in God rather than in your financial situation.

Fear has a way of blocking your miracle. A man came to Jesus one day and asked Him to come and pray for his little girl. Jesus followed him, but on the way was stopped by a brave, little woman who crawled through the crowd to touch His garment. Her infirmity of twelve years was completely healed. While Jesus talked with her a servant came to the man and said, "Don't bother the Master anymore for your daughter is dead." Jesus turned to him and said, "Fear not..." Fear can block your miracle. Your confidence in your Heavenly Father's love for you can cause that miracle to manifest in your home. You will always defeat fear if you hold on to what Jesus has said. This man held tightly to Jesus' words, *"Fear not..."* And, he joyfully received his precious daughter raised to life again. Jesus often said, *"Fear not."* God told Joshua, *"Fear not for I am with you."*

Fear stops many from obeying God, but it shouldn't be so. My father was an alcoholic while I was growing up. My mother shared a lot of things with me, not because I had any wisdom, but just because she had no one to talk to. When God called me to preach, I packed my few belongings, kissed my mother goodbye, kissed my little drunken daddy on his baldhead and walked out the door. Fear started to dog me. I pictured my mother sitting there crying. Fear said, "If you leave, she will just fall apart." The devil plagued me with lies, but I held onto the promise that said if I will faithfully serve the Lord, He would take care of my family. I didn't know how God was going to do it, but I believed that He would do it.

I was traveling in the ministry. Every Monday I sat down and wrote a letter to my mother to encourage her, and I went home as often as I could. After I left home, my daddy got worse and worse. The devil tried to get me to quit preaching by telling me to go back home. The devil told me that if I was there I could protect my mother. He kept trying to put fear in me by making me think I was responsible for my mother and my daddy. I did not fall to the devil's traps of fear. I obeyed God and dared to believe, and because I did not submit to fear, years later I was privileged to lead my daddy to the Lord.

The fear of the unknown is a kind of fear gripping people today. Elderly people are especially vulnerable to this kind of fear. They fear they won't be able to take care of themselves. They fear for their health and for their finances. Fear comes when you forget whose job it is to take care of you. It is not your job to take care of you. It is your Heavenly Father's job. He takes on the responsibility, and we should never make the mistake of taking that back from Him. We are safer in His hands than we are in our own hands. The fear of the unknown can be defeated if we remain confident in the Lord's willingness to care for us. He is loving and kind. He is faithful and true. We can rest assured of that.

Every time the Lord opens new doors of opportunity or ministry to you, you can write it down that the spirit of fear will come to torment. Before revival came in New Orleans, I went through a battle of fear that sometimes would almost paralyze me. It was indescribable fear. The devil tried to make me believe I would lose my ministry.

I was going through tremendous financial battles at the time in a business I owned. After we moved to New Orleans, I had started a little business and gave it over to a man I trusted to run it for me. Sometime later, he ran off and I discovered he had not been paying the bills. We owed literally thousands of dollars and had no money to pay our debts.

One day some of the most successful business people in the community called and asked me to have lunch with them. They said, "We need you to spearhead a program with the youth in New Orleans. If you will accept, we will set up a fund and pay your salary, expenses, furnish a car and home if you will leave your church and start working with the youth." They also wanted me to give up preaching about the Holy Spirit infilling with the evidence of tongues. I thanked them, but declined the offer.

The same week that I had lunch with these business people, my wife and two younger children had gone to see our parents in Arkansas. I came in from making hospital calls about one a.m. and saw my oldest son's light was still on, so I called to him and said, "Son, Dad's tired." I got into bed and had just dropped off to sleep when suddenly I felt an evil presence in my room. I began choking, trying to catch my breath. I jumped up. Standing at the foot of the bed was a black form about the size of a small man. Somehow in my confusion, I thought if I could get to the door and turn the overhead light on I would be all right. I started around the foot of the bed when this thing laughed at me and said, "You're going to lose your mind!" I stepped past it and reached for the light switch. As I fell to the floor face down, I heard myself speaking in tongues. I awoke at 5 a.m. I had sweated an outline of my body on the carpet. I was too weak to stand up so I crawled to the door, caught hold of the door frame and pulled myself up. Weak and trembling, I fell into bed.

Immediately I went into the most beautiful sleep. At 8:30 I heard my son moving around. I called to him and said, "Son, we've won! Go down to the business, lock it up and have the lights and phone turned off. We're through." We had won. I obeyed and the fear left.

I was so amazed. Why did I have such a peace even though my debts were still there? I owed an insurmountable amount of money. Every problem was still there, but incredible peace started flowing into my life.

The old man who owned the property where my business sat was on the committee that invented mean. He was just cruel. No kind words ever came out of his mouth. I knew that any day he could sue me for the money I owed him. Summer ended and fall came. I still had not heard from this man. On Thanksgiving Day in Dallas, I was preaching the state youth convention for the Assemblies of God. My family and I were eating in a restaurant when I was paged to go to the front for a phone call. It was my attorney who said, "Marvin, I just want to make your day. I just got a call from that old man's attorney. He has forgiven your total debt. He says you don't owe him anything!"

The fear that I went through, the battle I fought was against the devil trying to make me believe my finances would not work out and I would lose my mind. However, I can witness to you that if God speaks and you stay on course, you will come out victorious. God will give you victory. He is faithful to his children in spite of the difficulties they may go through. I knew the Lord had not released me from my church in New Orleans. I knew that He had not called me to accept the offer the businessmen had made. I desperately needed the money they offered, but I had to stay faithful to what God had said. When I did, God worked miracles on my behalf.

When Hurricane Katrina was raging, my wife and I were sitting in a hotel room watching it on television. I turned to her and quoted this verse, *"And we know that all things work together for good to those who love God, to those who are the called according to His purpose"* (Romans 8:28). This is one of the most powerful verses in the Bible. Do you believe it? If you do, your love for God can carry you through anything. Just believe and permit God to work on your behalf. Verse 29 helps us to know why these things are so. *"…to be conformed to His image…"* These things happened to cause me to be conformed to His image. He wants me to look like Him. He wants me to live without bitterness, without guile. He wants me to learn to be faithful through any adversity. He wants me to rest in the power of His love.

The Apostle Paul was a good father. He wrote to his spiritual son, Timothy, words of encouragement that still resonate in our hearts to this day. He was really saying, "I know something about fear, Timothy. You know for yourself the things I have survived. I know you are afraid, but here is what I have learned in my walk with Jesus Christ; the fear you are feeling was not sent by God. It was sent by the enemy to stop your work and destroy your faith. Timothy, if you will believe that God loves you, that He has not left you powerless, and that He is able to transform your mind by His Holy Scriptures, you will have good success."

Jesus paid with His own life for that good success Paul was talking about to Timothy. Paul went on to fearlessly become a partaker in that sacrifice as well, when he gave his life for the cause of Christ. He testified with his own life, *"Perfect love casts out fear."* Timothy, empowered by the love of God, went on to fulfill his mission to the early church.

CHAPTER SIX:
WORKING OUT YOUR SALVATION

Church pews are full of people who profess to be Christians and say they are saved. I differ and say the truth is they are being saved. They may be born again, and their sins may have been forgiven, but according to the scriptures they are being saved. They are working out their salvation. They have not yet accomplished it, and that is why they are having inner healing issues. If they were totally saved, they would have already conquered the works of the flesh. Instead, they are being saved. So am I.

"Therefore, my beloved, as you have always obeyed, not as in my presence only, but now much more in my absence, work out your own salvation with fear and trembling" (Philippians 2:12). The Apostle Paul was teaching a great truth to the church at Philippi. Being born again is no more the end of the matter than a baby being born is the end to life. It is the beginning. It is a thrilling, life-changing beginning, but it is not the end. There is much work to be done in between.

After an infant is born, he grows and learns, he makes mistakes and discovers new things, and he often mimics the adults around him. Have you ever seen a little one who wants to sweep the floor with his mother or drag around the leaf rake with his father? He discovers. He learns. He works. A two-year-old is more apt to want to work than a twelve-year-old. Everything is a discovery to him. Although he works and learns throughout his day, has he added one ounce by his own efforts to the fact that he belongs to his mother and father? By the end of the day when he lays his little head on his pillow, has he become more of a son? Of course not! I am not saying that working out your salvation makes you become more of a son to your Heavenly Father. I am saying that working out your salvation will make you act more like a loving son to your Heavenly Father. That is what Paul was teaching the church at Philippi.

There is a lot of working in and a lot of working out in this Christian walk. Have you ever worked fertilizer into the soil you want to improve? You mix this rich addition into the poor, thin soil, and the next thing you know, you're slicing open a fat, juicy tomato for your lunch. There is a working into the life of a Christian that takes place. There is also a working out of the life that takes place. Take that same patch of soil and you may have to run your hoe through it and pick out all the rocks. If you live in the Missouri Ozarks you have to take a pry bar to the rocks! There is a working out that takes place.

In the Christian's life, faith and truth have to be worked in while sin and lies have to be worked out. For some, a pry bar is needed to pry up the lies and sins. Nothing good will grow in that person's life until the working out is done. Sin has to go. Did you know that Satan would have no control over you whatsoever if it was not for sin? When Adam fell by willfully sinning, he opened the door for demonic forces to attack him. Up until the fall, Adam and Eve were not walking around doing spiritual warfare. When they sinned, Satan swooped in with all sorts of attacks.

Understanding this should help you realize that the thing giving you problems and the fact that you are allowing Satan to harass you is because of what is in you. Jesus said Satan could do nothing to Him because he had nothing in Him. Does that make sense to you? So when we begin to think in terms of demonic activity and Satan harassing us, we need to check our lives. When we commit a sin, that opens the door for Satan to begin to harass us.

We also have to understand that Satan attacks us because of who we are. We belong to Jesus Christ. That automatically makes us the enemy. A soldier serving in the Armed Forces is not confused when the enemy attacks. He knows that is not only expected, but anticipated. The soldier's job is to defend himself and others against the attack. However, it is a very foolish soldier indeed who leaves the door open to his barracks and then wonders why the enemy creeps inside. Christians need to understand there may be things in their lives that open the door to demonic attacks. Ignorance can open the door to satanic attacks. In Hosea, the prophet lamented, *"My people are destroyed for lack of knowledge."* In other words, their ignorance was killing them.

A common misconception in the world often carries over into the church. It says that people are basically good. The truth is that without Jesus Christ changing and transforming our hearts and minds, we are just as capable of doing evil as the next guy. How many of us have been astonished by reports of priests, pastors, deacons and Sunday school teachers doing unimaginable things to little children? King David understood this. *"Behold, I was brought forth in iniquity, and in sin my mother conceived me"* (Psalm 51:5). Was David admitting his mother had been unfaithful to her husband? Of course not! He was recognizing the iniquity that is inherent in us all.

Iniquity is when a person is bent, crooked or has a tendency toward certain wrong things. David said, *"From my mother's womb I was bent in a certain direction going away from God."* Rebellion is inherent in every person. Mothers know this to be so, especially when their two-year-old is pulling against them in the grocery store hollering, "No!" This natural rebellion and sin nature is in each of us and must be worked out of our lives.

Right now I can see some people silently arguing with me. "Brother Gorman doesn't understand," they are saying to themselves. "I was abused by others. I was wounded. I was maligned. I was accused." That may be true, and I am very sorry for it. However, the trouble is not really what happened to you, but how you are dealing with what happened to you. I understand that you may not have had any control over what happened. Your husband may have attacked you. Your wife may have cheated on you. Your parents may have abused or neglected you. You had no control over that. As a born again Christian though, you do have control over what you do about it. That is where you can choose to sin or not. Your choice will determine what Satan can do to you.

Have you ever been around property that had signs posted, "Keep out!" Satan has to operate according to God's laws of authority. He cannot just automatically jump on someone. He had no access into Adam and Eve's lives until he convinced them to fall for a lie and sin against God. If a Christian opens himself up to thoughts that are evil, to imaginations that are evil and activities that are evil, that gives Satan a legal right to gain access. Evil thoughts don't come from God! They come from Satan, so when you have his property, he has a right to attack you.

Our social and cultural upbringing can open the door to satanic attack. My father was an alcoholic, so as a small child I felt the sting of being a social outcast. Add to that the fact that both my mother and father were partially of Native American descent and I grew up in an era of time when it wasn't fashionable to be Native American. From the time I was in second grade until I was born again, I can't remember going to school without being in at least one fistfight a day. Sometimes it was two or three fistfights. I was so angry I would fight a boy or a girl. If I was crossed, I'd fight. I also had a tongue that could scalp you in a minute. That was my defense, a fistfight or my sharp tongue. I felt angry because I knew I was being socially rejected.

I later thought, "Well that's just the way Gormans are." My grandfather was a German-Jew who married a Cherokee. My daddy married a lady of Choctaw descent, so I just couldn't help it. I was German-Jew-Cherokee-Choctaw. No wonder I liked to fight! I was bent in that direction. My social and cultural upbringing caused me to open a lot of doors that I later had to learn to close. I was a teenager when I was born again. I had a lot to do as I worked out my salvation. I had to close some doors in order to break bondages.

Man is controlled and held in bondage by whatever he allows to possess him. The Apostle Peter warned, *"While they promise them liberty, they themselves are slaves of corruption; for by whom a person is overcome, by him also he is brought into bondage"* (II Peter 2:19).

A man is a slave to whatever controls him. Have you ever seen a pack of cigarettes crack the whip and up jumps the man to run out to light one up? Have you ever seen a box of donuts crack the whip and up jumps the Christian to gobble them down and overdose on sugar for the day? Have you ever seen a woman in bondage to bitterness? Have you ever seen a man in bondage to anger and wrath? A man is a slave to whatever controls him.

It might be cigarettes and donuts today, but drugs and alcohol tomorrow. Then it may grow to lust and perversion the next day, and before it's all over the Christian is sitting in jail wondering how in the world his life has come to this. Sin begets sin. Sin lays wide open the door for demonic activity.

The reason we can be put into bondage by Satan is because of our carnal nature and our fleshly nature. Every one of us was born into this world a sinner. A little baby seems as innocent as he can be, but he was also born into sin. He won't have to learn how to be a sinner. He is a sinner. He is not going to have to learn how to lie. When he gets a little older he'll just lie. He'll have to be delivered from that. He won't have to be taught how to be selfish. He'll just automatically say, "Mine!" He won't have to be taught how to lose his temper, he'll just do it. All of that is part of the fall in the Garden of Eden. When that child comes to the age of accountability, he will personally have to repent of his sins and accept Jesus Christ as his Savior.

Some Christians believe that when they prayed the sinner's prayer their carnal nature was suddenly changed. But many of us know Christians whose anger still has them in bondage. We may have been born again, but we have to work out our salvation. We must attack these things and work on them until they are defeated.

How many of you have had problems with temper and anger since you were born again? Evidently it did not all go away when you were born again, did it? How many of you have had problems with jealousy? How many have had problems with envy? How many of you have had problems with other fleshly things? These are things that prevent you from living a victorious life. All of these things grieve the Holy Spirit, and if the Holy Spirit is being grieved, these things must be dealt with and conquered. If they are not dealt with and conquered, then how can the Holy Spirit lead us? Only those led by the Spirit of God are the sons of God.

You become corrupt by lust and desires that are prompted by delusions. Satan makes you believe what you are doing is not bad. Paul instructed the church at Ephesus to, "*Strip yourselves of your former nature [put off and discard your old unrenewed self which characterized your previous manner of life and becomes corrupt through lusts and desires that spring from delusion*" (Ephesians 4:22, AMP).

One day I was attempting to help a couple work their way through a situation in which they had been deeply hurt. I was coaching them to forgive. They finally agreed to forgive the offending party. So I said, "Here's what you do then, whenever you talk to them next just say to them, 'Look, I realize that I was wrong, and said some things that were wrong, and acted in a manner that was grievous to the Spirit, but I am asking you to forgive me.'" When I began counseling in this manner, one of them spoke up and said, "Why should I have to be the one who says that? They are the ones who hurt me!" I said, "Because if you want to be healed then you must release that." They sputtered and spit asking, "Why can't they be the first to do it?" I answered, "They probably could, but what is keeping you from doing it?"

Pride and anger are inseparable twin sisters. Anywhere you have a lot of anger you also have pride. I counseled this couple because of their feelings of being hurt by another Christian couple. It wasn't long until they became indignant, then angry. Then pride came swooping in to entice them to stumble. Once I helped them work their way through this, they humbled themselves and repented to the other couple. God helped them, they obeyed Him, and they enjoyed victory! Many marriages get into deep trouble because each one knows that the other one wronged them, so they wait on the other person to repent. Pride and anger eats away their lives.

Our Father didn't model this behavior. He loved us so much even when we were wrong. Our parents knew we were wrong. Even every angel knew we were wrong, yet God sent His beloved son to us anyway. We didn't come to Him, He came to us. We didn't choose Him, He chose us. He forgave us. "While we were yet in sin Christ died for us," Paul wrote. He took upon Himself all of our sin while we were yet in sin and He died for the ungodly. The servant is not greater than the master. We must lay down our pride and be the first to forgive. Every time we wait for someone else to come to us, we are robbing ourselves of victory. Forgive! Be the first to forgive and mean it from your heart.

This is what the Apostle Paul was referring to when he said, "Put off the old man." Throughout that passage Paul kept talking about the mind. Renew the mind. Then he said "strip off the old man." How are you going to strip off the old man? You need to strip off the old way of thinking in order to begin thinking differently.

Paul knew what he was talking about to the church in Corinth when he said, "Take every thought and every imagination that is contrary to God and bring it under subjection." In other words, make those thoughts bow down and line up with the Word of God. Your mind must be renewed because all of us war with the Adamic nature.

All of us started out with wrong thinking. Our thinking has to be reprogrammed. A lot of people grew up in families with moms and dads who influenced them to think things that were a hindrance to them. When they come to God, they bring those wrong mindsets. My mother was part Choctaw. She was very superstitious and fearful. All of us kids picked up on that so we became very superstitious and fearful. When I was born again, I started working to rid myself of those fears and those superstitions. I determined I didn't want my little children to grow up thinking that way. The way you think is powerful, so your mind has to be renewed.

Some parents teach their children that God's love is dependent on their actions. I've heard parents say that to their children. They grow up having trouble believing that God really loves them. The truth is God loves them no matter what they do. Haven't we all wanted our children to memorize John 3:16? He loves us no matter what we do, but He loved us so much He sent Jesus for us so that we would stop destroying our own lives with what we have been doing! As we grow in our Christian faith, we have to learn new ways of thinking which line up with the Word of God.

We also have to learn new ways of acting. Our behavior will change when our thinking processes change. When we start out in this life our very nature is against us, working contrary to the works of the Holy Spirit. Paul had to work very hard to get this point across to the church at Galatia. They wanted to call themselves Christians, but their behavior was anything but Christ-like. A majority of people in America today call themselves Christians, but many are a million miles away from Christ-like behavior. A Hindu priest in India once said, "If Christians lived what Jesus Christ taught, no one would want to remain a Hindu."

Paul was trying to get the Church to practice what they professed. *"Now the doings (practices) of the flesh are clear (obvious): they are immorality, impurity, indecency, idolatry, sorcery, enmity, strife, jealousy, anger (ill temper), selfishness, divisions (dissensions), party spirit (factions, sects with peculiar opinions, heresies), envy, drunkenness, carousing, and the like. I*

112

warn you beforehand, just as I did previously, that those who do such things shall not inherit the kingdom of God" (Galatians 5:19-21, AMP). Paul admitted that our very nature is against us and practicing sin opens the door for Satan to have a right to harass us.

If unchanged, our very nature produces sexual immorality, impure thoughts, eagerness for lustful pleasures, idolatry, participation in demonic activity, hostility, quarreling, jealousy, outbursts of anger, selfish ambition, division and feelings that everyone is wrong except those in our little group. We must admit that everybody is born that way. It is just a natural thing, unless we deal with that and work it out of our lives. When you allow something into your life which comes from the devil such as envy, lying, selfishness or unforgiveness, you must believe Satan is coming to claim what is his. His property can be accessed by him at will. If he wants to pitch a tent and stay, he can and he surely will. Sin opens the door.

When I was a kid my mother kept plenty of food in our house. We raised almost all of our food. Mother was a good cook. She always saw that we had plenty to eat. We were never denied the right to go to the fridge, or the warmer and get some food. She made extra biscuits in the morning because we played hard and got hungry. We would run into the kitchen to eat those leftover biscuits with sweet preserves or raw honey. Mother never told us we couldn't eat them, but she always told us not to drip the preserves or honey on the cabinet or counter. "If you do the ants will come," she warned. How an ant in the middle of the field knows when honey is dripping down the side of a jar in the kitchen, I'll never know! Next thing you know we would see a trail of ants coming and going around that cabinet. My brothers and I used to take our thumbs and mash the ants, but ten more would be in line heading for the honey jar. But the moment we washed the side of the jar and wiped down the cabinet the ants left.

Do you have demonic forces oppressing your life? Wash off the container and wipe down the cabinet. Demons don't hang around trying to feed off of righteousness, peace and joy in the Holy Ghost!

That's why you have to work out your salvation and put the old man to death. The old carnal nature has to die. You have to choose to crucify it. Have you ever heard it said, "I'm only doing what comes naturally?" We laugh at that many times, but that's true. According to the scripture it is natural for people to act like animals. Without Christ in their life that's what they do. The animalistic nature we have fights against us and if left unchanged will ultimately destroy us.

Have you ever become disgusted with yourself and asked, "Now where did that thought come from? That's not me!" That is you without Christ. That is you without renewing your mind! Without a conscious effort to change your way of thinking, there is an eagerness for lustful pleasures. Several years ago an instrument was developed which you could attach to your television to block out the curse words. One day my friend and I were talking to someone about a certain movie they had watched. My friend asked this guy how many curse words were in the movie. The man replied, 'Oh, at least five or six." My friend replied, "How about 30?" We have been so desensitized to cursing on television that we hear it, but no longer pay attention to it. We can be sure however, little children can hear it.

Unfortunately, it is in our human nature to tolerate that kind of stuff. That is why we need the renewing of our minds. We also need the renewing of our hearts. Jesus said, *"For out of the heart proceed evil thoughts, murders, adulteries, fornications, thefts, false witness, blasphemies. These are the things which defile a man, but to eat with unwashed hands does not defile a man"* (Matthew 15:19-20). Our heart has more to do than just pump blood through our bodies. It has much to do with our thinking. Solomon wrote, *"For as he thinks in his heart, so is he..."* (Proverbs 23:7a). Murder, adultery, fornication, theft, false witnesses and blasphemies come out of your unregenerate thought life. Without Christ, that is what each of us is capable of doing. That is why our hearts and our minds have to be submitted to the Word of God and the Spirit of God for a complete change. Those who shook the pastor's hand and joined the church cannot rely on that sort of business transaction to make them a Christian. Being a Christian means being like Jesus Christ.

If the body of Christ today could understand the power they have to create change, we would constantly be rejoicing. The very fact that you are learning to think differently and act differently as born again believers serving a true and living God can affect your home and your community. You affect your family when your way of thinking becomes more Christ-like. You can also affect it in a negative way. If one member of your family in your home is upset and angry, doesn't that affect your home and your whole family? If mama is on the rampage, doesn't that make everybody nervous? If daddy comes in angry because he has had a bad day at the office or on the job, doesn't that upset everybody? He may not have to say anything, perhaps it is just the way he closes the door. By that you know you must walk softly. Bad tempers have the power to effect change. In the same way, Christ-like behavior has the power to effect change. Sin and those given over to carnal natures may be all around us, but we can still choose what we will think and what we will permit in our hearts. Those choices have the power to bring about wonderful changes in families and communities.

When we get our minds renewed, our patterns of thinking change, so that our conversations will also change. Your mind, will and emotions are valuable. If they're under the influence of the wrong force, they can be detrimental, but if they're under the influence of the right force, they can be powerful in bringing victory and deliverance. Jesus said what defiles a man is what he speaks or declares. We will be judged for what we say. Jesus said, *"For by your words you will be justified, and by your words you will be condemned"* (Matthew 12:37). If you don't get your thinking straight and your heart straight by working out your salvation, then your fleshly nature will begin to cause you to say things that are harmful.

I can choose to speak blessings or I can speak curses on you. People who are in authority can literally destroy you with their words. There are families that are torn apart because of the way the husband speaks. There are children whose lives are warped because of the way they have been spoken to in the home. "You'll never amount to anything. You're a bad kid!" some parents say.

I would have a hard time staying calm if I ever heard someone telling my grandkids they are bad. They've never been told that. I tell them how wonderful they are. I tell them how proud I am of them. I tell them what great potential they have. I tell them how God is going to use them one day. I'm speaking that into their lives constantly because words are powerful. Some of you are hurting, not because somebody came along and hit you with their fist or hit you with a club, but they spoke a word to you that cut inside of you. You're having difficulty getting healed from words that were spoken. We must have our hearts and our thinking changed so that our words will be kind and good toward others.

Many have purposed in their heart to never tell a lie again, but before you know it, a lie has come out of their mouth. It's their sin nature working against them. You have to understand that you have to crucify that old man. This is not something that is going to go away on its own. That is why it is called "working out your salvation."

"Oh, Brother Gorman I got saved and I was slain in the Spirit!" Honey, you can be slain in the Spirit every time you come to church and it's not going to deliver you from that old carnal nature. That old man has to die. He must be crucified. Nobody can lay hands on you and make it right. Your pastor can rub you bald-headed praying for you so much, but that won't cure you. You have to take your sin nature by the throat, and you must deal with it by the Word of God and by prayer until it is dead.

I've listened to people tell me, "Oh, I'm saved and filled with the Holy Ghost! I just automatically changed." If that is true, wonderful! However, more than likely you will have to retrain your mind and heart just like the rest of us. Paul addressed this matter with the church at Corinth. *"I thank my God always concerning you for the grace of God which was given to you by Christ Jesus, that you were enriched in everything by Him in all utterance and all knowledge, even as the testimony of Christ was confirmed in you, so that you come short in no gift, eagerly waiting for the revelation of our Lord Jesus Christ"* (I Corinthians 1:4-7). He began his letter by loving on the people and affirming them. They were baptized in the Holy Spirit. They had spiritual gifts in operation, but there was a problem. He told them they were not spiritual. *"And I, brethren, could not speak to you as to spiritual people but as to carnal, as to babes in Christ. I fed you with milk and not with solid food; for until now you were not able to receive it, and even now you are still not able; for you are still carnal. For where there are envy, strife, and divisions among you, are you not carnal and behaving like mere men?"* (I Corinthians 3:1-3).

They had all the gifts. It was the same crowd, the same church he was just talking to moments ago, but then he said he had to talk to them as babes, *"for you are yet carnal."* How did he know they were carnal? He knew they were born again because of their utterance, their knowledge, and confirmation of their testimony, but he said, *"The reason I know you are carnal is there is among you envy, strife and division."* The scripture says, *"Where there is envy and jealousy, there's every evil work."*

How many know people in your church who are envious? These same people may talk in tongues, lay hands on others and even see others healed. But just because you are born again and filled with the Spirit does not mean that you have conquered the carnal nature. You may know people who are critical, backbiting, gossipers, saved and filled with the Holy Spirit. There are those who have unforgiveness in their hearts. They may have gone through a bitter divorce, and dragged their children through divorce. They cannot forgive the man or woman that they were married to because of what they put them through, and yet they are born again, speak with tongues, and many times are involved with church. Many are so filled with anger; you have to walk on eggshells around them or they will explode. That is what has brought the church to where it is today. We have dealt with the blessing, but we haven't dealt with crucifying the old man. If Christ is going to be Lord of our lives then we must crucify the flesh, and allow the Word of God and the Spirit of God to rule our lives.

Do you think the Holy Spirit and the angels are eager to minister to you whenever you are filled with anger? What kind of spirit do you think comes to you then? Evil spirits are drawn to you. What kind of spirit is drawn to you when somebody is talking against a brother or sister? Someone says, "No demons are bothering me!" Honey, they are sleeping with you! They are being drawn. I didn't say they are in you, but are around you trying to orchestrate your life.

Something has to be done if we're going to be the church that will rise up to devastate the strong man. How can a person continue to cast out devils when they have demons all around them because of anger, unforgiveness, bitterness, or a hypocritical spirit? How can they expect to chase the devil away?

If we allow our carnal nature to be in control, we will be oppressed and attacked, so we must work out our salvation. Working out my salvation is not talking in tongues. That's a gift.

I have to start concentrating on fruit. The thing that will make me what I really want to be, give me peace, and move me into a position where Satan cannot harass me, is when I am so deeply into the love of Christ that I will not tolerate in me anything that does not look like Him. I have to close every door to Satan and open the door to Jesus.

Christians will never get there until they deal with things in them. They are going to have to learn how to repent. If you haven't repented today you may very well be spiritually soiled. There are things working against your spiritual life that will get you down if you haven't repented today. Repentance washes away all the old and causes you to stand in the presence of the Lord clean and pure.

When you repent, you crucify the old man. Repentance is what crucifies him. He wants you to get mad, but you repent and say, "God, I am sorry that I even had the thought of getting angry. I'm sorry I had a sharp tongue. I'm repenting, so God, please pour your love into me." When I treat someone badly, it isn't what is in him that makes me treat him badly. It's what is in me. Have you ever heard the saying, "That person brings the worst out in me?" What if there was no worst in you? You can't bring out what is not in you! That's what repentance does. It takes the worst out and allows the Holy Spirit to put in the best.

Working out your salvation won't make you anymore born again, but it will bring you into a place of peace with God, with others and with your own conscience. Working out your salvation will make you more Christ-like. It will keep you from providing footholds for Satan in your life where he can drag you back into sin. Working out your salvation will close the doors to Satan, and it will keep you from damaging yourself and others.

Working out your salvation is an act of your own will. When you are born again, you have to choose to submit to the work of Christ in your life, through a lifestyle of repentance. By that, you toss out the old man on his ear, you free yourself from carnal lusts and desires, and you begin to shine like Jesus shines.

A woman once asked me, "What kind of sins can I commit and still make it to heaven?" I thought about it for a moment then responded, "What if a woman had fallen deeply in love with a handsome man and married him? What if this man was truly wonderful to her? He brought her gifts, washed her car, never forgot her birthday and showered her with love and affection. He was always attentive and courteous. He always opened her car door and treated her like a princess. He always spoke to his friends about her in glowing terms of love and adoration. He knew her better than anyone on the face of the earth and still thought she was amazing. He carried her when she was weak. He allowed her gifts and strengths to grow and flourish. Whatever she needed, he was able to give. Now suppose a man at work began to try to catch her eye. He was always in the break room when she was. He was always trying to get her to talk to him. He even hinted to her about having an affair with him. How close to him could she get without it being sin?" The woman looked at me with a frown, "Why would she want to? Her husband is so perfect!" I waited for her own words to sink into her soul. "Oh," she exhaled, "I get it."

Why would anyone want to accommodate sin in their lives when their Savior Jesus Christ has loved them so perfectly? Falling in love with Christ will cause you to eagerly work out your salvation, slamming shut the door to Satan and removing you far from his control.

CHAPTER SEVEN:
TRANSFERENCE OF SPIRITS

A clever deception of the enemy is misleading Christian families today. Somehow they believe they are immune from the corrupting influences of family, friends, movies, television, books and magazines. Just because a person is a Christian doesn't mean he cannot be twisted and perverted from the truth of life in Jesus Christ. The Apostle Paul heard about a perversion that was happening in the church at Corinth. Believers had been taken in by an insidious teaching that Christ did not literally rise from the dead. In fact, this damaging teaching included that no one rises from the dead. Paul replied, If, in the manner of men, I have fought with beasts at Ephesus, what advantage is it to me? If the dead do not rise, *"Let us eat and drink, for tomorrow we die!" Do not be deceived: "Evil company corrupts good habits"* (I Cor. 15:32-33.) The Amplified Bible phrases it, *"Do not be so deceived and misled! Evil companionships (communion, associations) corrupt and deprave good manners and morals and character."* Paul was telling the church, "You are hanging around with the wrong people. They have pulled you away from the truth." This same deception works today.

In our rush to be accommodating to the world, we have tried to look like them, walk like them and talk like them. We are afraid our righteousness will make their unrighteousness look bad so we have lowered our standards so as not to appear legalistic. It is not legalistic to dress modestly. Unfortunately, some folks believe that by modestly covering our bodies, we are being legalistic. That's not true at all. Instead, we are trying to be a good role model for true Christian character. True Christian character does not prompt members of the opposite sex to lustful thoughts.

If you're not careful and you begin running with the wrong crowd, you will begin to think less about true Christian character, and more about fashion or fitting in with everyone else. A Christian is not necessarily supposed to fit in. He is supposed to understand that this world is not his home. We are strangers and sojourners, as we just pass through this temporary life to the life that is eternal.

If a Christian begins to hang around the wrong people, he will find there is such a thing as transference of spirits. I have heard Christians say they don't believe there is such a thing as transference of spirits. I guarantee you that, if they thought about it, every mother would believe such a thing. If there are bad kids in your neighborhood and your children run around with them, suddenly you are dealing with rebellion, anger, lying, cheating and stealing. Your kids act and react according to what is working in another child.

Many a young person was destroyed because they went to a rock concert and just wanted to be accepted by the crowd. Soon, they were hostile against their parents, dealing with evil on every side and sneaking around so they could drink and smoke. Why? They opened themselves up to evil spirits at the concert, and they came home a changed person. It happens in daycares too. You can watch your child's actions and reactions and tell when they have been with rebellious children who have not been properly trained and disciplined.

Your child comes home whining, fussing and throwing tantrums because his little spirit has been hindered by what was influencing that other child.

People will listen to a Christian recording and remark how wonderful it made them feel in their spirits. Those same people will listen to a trashy rock or rap recording and say it hasn't affected their spirits at all. Youth pastors have a saying today: garbage in—garbage out. What you listen to you become. When we begin to open ourselves up to that which we know is unwholesome and does not edify, we are open to the transference of evil spirits.

We need to understand the words coming out of us must edify and build up our spirit man. How many times have we heard someone say how powerful music is? Words are powerful. Coupled with music, they are doubly powerful. When I was a kid, I heard the schoolyard rhyme, "Sticks and stones may break my bones, but words will never hurt me." The truth is words did hurt me. If someone said I was worthless because my daddy was an alcoholic, those words went deep into my spirit and formed anger inside of me that I had to deal with decades later. We have to be careful what we allow our ears to hear because that is what forms our thought processes.

Perhaps a man has really been pressing into God, but on the job he starts hanging around with the wrong men; eating lunch with them, talking, communicating and associating. If he is not careful to guard his thought life, their evil ways will begin to affect him.

I know people I will not associate with because they want to tell shady jokes. The Bible says, "Out of the abundance of the heart, the mouth speaks." Don't open yourself up to what is in their hearts. Evil spirits are expert at drawing individuals into thinking and speaking wrong things. Some women go out to eat with other women, sit and talk, and the first thing you know they would rather be with the gals than with the man they married. Some men would rather be with men in the bar rooms or pool halls than with their own wife. There is something wrong with that. Hanging out with guys who have wicked spirits on them can cause those spirits to transfer to you bringing real trouble into your marriage.

I believe one of the basic causes of divorce in America is trashy soap operas. Christians should never watch such garbage. We have to be careful what we set before our eyes. Ever notice how all the characters on the soap operas are well-shaped, well-dressed, wealthy, and powerful; and they always seem to have just the right line to say? The Christian lady's poor husband comes home from the office where his boss has chewed on him, his co-worker chewed on him and the guy at the lunch counter chewed on him. His deodorant has long since stopped working, and he hasn't brushed his teeth since he left the house that morning. He comes home and all he wants is to get a hug and kiss. He wants her to affirm him and tell him that he is smart and valuable. Instead, she shrugs him off and mentally compares him with Mister Soap Star, whose tanned, handsome face is flawless, whose wardrobe is impeccable and whose breath she will never have to deal with. The next thing you know, her husband just can't measure up. She lives in a fantasy world where her husband is not welcome to join. She files for divorce.

I was counseling with a couple that had been influenced by these soap operas. I counseled the wife to go cold turkey and stop her addiction to those shows. Then I counseled her to spend that same amount of time in the study of the scriptures in vital communication with the Lord. She did, and the result was her husband suddenly became much more attractive to her than he had ever been before.

What we set before our eyes seriously determines who we will become. Have you ever noticed someone who commits hideous sex crimes against children? What do the police always find in his house? There will always be filthy magazines, or DVDs or child pornography on the computer. As he feeds on this wickedness, he is opened for transference of evil spirits. Very soon those evil spirits entice him to act out what he has been looking at. He never set out to be a sexual predator, but what he set before his eyes overtook his heart and mind.

Samson learned about transference of spirits the hard way, and paid the price for it with his life. Samson was the star of the soap operas in his day. He was the strongest, most handsome Nazarene in Israel. Israel had again done evil in the sight of the Lord, so God had permitted the Philistines to take them into captivity for a period of forty years. In the midst of this terrible political and social situation, an angel came to a little lady who had been barren. The cry of her heart was for a child. The angel promised to her and to her husband, Manoah, a son who would begin to deliver Israel out of the hands of the Philistines.

When Samson was a young man, he was strong, but impetuous and spoiled. The devil knew that because he is a real pro at focusing his attacks on our areas of weakness. Samson's weakness was women. In the Valley of Sorek, he fell in love with a woman named Delilah. The Philistines enticed her to use her feminine wiles to discover the secret of his great strength. Three times she thought he had told her the true story of his strength only to find that he was mocking her. In Judges 16:16-17, we can easily see the method most often used by the devil. *"And it came to pass, when she pestered him daily with her words and pressed him, so that his soul was vexed to death, that he told her all his heart, and said to her, 'No razor has ever come upon my head, for I have been a Nazirite to God from my mother's womb. If I am shaven, then my strength will leave me, and I shall become weak, and be like any other man.'"* His uncut hair, his long, black locks were the key to his unfathomable strength. She lulled him to sleep on her lap and had a conspirator slip in shaving off the seven locks of his head. His strength left him. Evil company corrupts good habits. Paul was right. Samson's one true love betrayed him for money, and taunted him when his strength was gone.

The Philistines easily captured him and gouged out his eyes. They bound him with bronze fetters making him a grinder at the prison. You have a lot of time to think when you can't see anything and all you do all day long is walk around and around in circles. Perhaps for the first time Samson could really see. Perhaps for the first time he remembered his parents warning him about the company he was keeping. He realized that he had given himself over to spirits other than the Holy Spirit. His soap opera good looks were gone. No one was waiting to ask for his autograph and in fact, they soon began to forget him. That was their undoing.

The hair of his head began to grow again. How silly of the Philistines to forget! They only remembered him when the lords of the Philistines gathered together to offer a great sacrifice to Dagon, their god, and to rejoice. Wine flowed like water making everyone reckless and foolish as wine always does. They called for Samson to be brought out to entertain them. What kind of entertainment were they anticipating? Samson was about to put on a show that would bring the house down. He asked the young boy who led him by the hand to help him place his hands on the pillars which supported the temple so that he could lean on them. He did lean on them with the mighty infusion of strength that came by the power of the Holy Spirit in answer to his prayer. He brought the temple down in one thunderous moment. Three thousand people and one soap opera star died that day.

Evil companionships corrupt and deprave good manners, morals and character. Samson learned that lesson the hard way. That's why it is so difficult for me to understand why Christian parents today indulge their children and turn a blind eye when they see their children seeking after worldly pleasures and friendships. Do their children have to learn the hard way too? Evil spirits look for opportunities to transfer to others and propagate their evil deeds.

When a Christian understands this fact, he should break off associations with others who want them to continue in sin. It is absolutely necessary for Christians to measure carefully their associations with non-believers. We need to be salt and light to the world, but sometimes our spiritual strength is not what Jesus' was when He sat down to eat with publicans and sinners. Just because Jesus did so does not mean we are ready to do so without being pulled back to sinful behaviors.

In Deuteronomy, Moses recorded the laws concerning going out to war. God was being very specific with Moses and the children of Israel for a reason. He knew the demons that operated behind the false gods who inhabited the Promised Land were not going to just pack their bags and move out. They were going to tempt the children of Israel to fall back into sin. In Deuteronomy 20:16, God ordered, *"But of the cities of these peoples which the LORD your God gives you as an inheritance, you shall let nothing that breathes remain alive."* In verse 18, God makes it perfectly clear why He made this order. *"…lest they teach you to do according to all their abominations which they have done for their gods, and you sin against the LORD your God."*

God said for them to kill the cattle, beasts and every human. He commanded them to save none of them alive. "Utterly destroy them!" He commanded. I used to have problems with that until I understood what God wanted. God was not a blood-thirsty being who wanted to kill people. God is a good Father who wants to protect His children. God was willing to sacrifice entire countries for Israel. He was willing to fight for His people. He knew that from the heathen people who worshiped false gods, there would be the transference of spirits to His children. The spirits would cause them to conform to the worship of idol gods. He knew the only thing to do was wipe these people out because their devotion to false gods was so strong, and the spirits associated with them would cause His people to go into error. Was God correct in thinking that would happen?

Solomon was known as the wisest man who ever lived. He was permitted by God to build an extravagant temple. He was given by God unmatched wealth, but I Kings 11:4 records a sad fact. *"For it was so, when Solomon was old, that his wives turned his heart after other gods; and his heart was not loyal to the LORD his God, as was the heart of his father David."* His seven hundred wives convinced him to permit the worship of Ashtoreth, Milcom (or Molech), and Chemosh. These were some of the same gods the Canaanites had been worshiping centuries earlier when God helped the Israelites drive them out because of the very fact they were worshiping these abominations. If the wisest man who ever lived, and who experienced the power and presence of God in the temple, could later be falsely persuaded--don't believe for a moment that you should take any chances!

Some Christians come out of a relationship that included receiving personal gifts such as jewelry and photos. It is often necessary to get rid of these physical items before the emotional and spiritual attachments can be severed, especially if the relationship was sexual. Examine the gifts or objects you have received from others, asking the Lord if there are any that could cause you to be drawn back to a life of sin.

When I served as a pastor in New Orleans, often during revival services the altar area would be littered with packages of cigarettes, drugs and drug paraphernalia, gold chains, jewelry and music tapes from those who had been set free and wanted to stay free.

You also need to examine jewelry, trinkets, what-nots and other treasured possessions left to you by family members. I ministered to a lady one time who treasured a necklace which had been passed down in her family. I asked her, "Where did you get that beautiful necklace?" She told me that it belonged to her grandmother. I said to her, "Honey, you know your grandmother was the meanest soul on the street. She never had a kind word to say, she was critical, domineering and talked to your grandpa like he was dirt. She never treated him with respect. Now this is the treasured possession you are clinging to? Why?" She knew what I said was true. She was often the brunt of her grandmother's meanness. Sometime later she came back to me and said, "I got to thinking about what you said. I pitched that necklace. I didn't want that mean spirit to start trying to harass me." I knew she had a Biblical precedent for this.

When the children of Israel conquered Jericho, they killed everything that lived, just as the Lord had commanded. But one Israelite helped himself to a heap of trouble. Joshua 7:1 records, *"But the children of Israel committed a trespass regarding the accursed things, for Achan the son of Carmi, the son of Zabdi, the son of Zerah, of the tribe of Judah, took of the accursed things; so the anger of the LORD burned against the children of Israel."* After a stunning defeat at the battle of Ai, Joshua threw himself on the ground and pleaded with God to know why. God told him to get up and do something about it. He informed Joshua that someone in the camp had taken of the accursed thing. Finally, Achan was confronted and confessed that when he saw among the spoils a beautiful Babylonian garment, two hundred shekels of silver, and a wedge of gold of 50 shekels' weight, he coveted them and took them. For these items both Achan and his entire family lost their lives that day. Achan's actions brought a curse on the whole nation of Israel and a defeat at Ai. Israel stoned him and every single thing that he had including his family and livestock, and then burned them with all his possessions. The law he violated was meted out against him. Why? God didn't want the spirits associated with the Canaanites to invade the Israelites. God's actions may seem harsh until you consider all the weeping wives and children of the men needlessly slaughtered in the battle of Ai because of Achan's selfish sin. God shut the door so that evil spirits could not transfer to His children.

In the book of Acts, Luke wrote about a remarkable revival with many people delivered from all sorts of witchcrafts and sorceries. The result was the people of the city took all the evil books and burned them. Why? You need to watch what you have in your home. I was in Mexico preaching a ministers' conference when a lady came up and handed me a coin. In that country the least value the coin has, the bigger it is in size. Their biggest coins are worth less than a half cent. She gave me this beautiful, shiny coin. This happened after the service. The offering unto the Lord had already been received. Later when we were in the car, my missionary host said to me, "If you keep that coin, be careful and if strange things start to happen to you, pitch it out or destroy it." He had been there eighteen years in the ministry. He knew by hard experience the people given to witchcraft would try to control or disrupt by getting the victim to take a beautiful object with a curse on it. Then the curse would come on him. I pitched the coin out the window.

Some modern Christians don't believe in such a thing. Let me remind you the devil hasn't gotten any nicer just because we have more modern things in our lives. Why was it that when Hezekiah cleansed the temple he destroyed many things? Old Ahab had been drinking out of the items that had been consecrated to the Lord. Hezekiah knew those spirits that had operated in Ahab were attached to those items. Satan worshipers love to take items that were dedicated or consecrated to God and desecrate them. If a person was to go into a place of Satanic worship, without exception something precious to the Christian body will be there. It might be a chalice, communion set, cross or any number of things which they desecrate. They pronounce curses over them which can cause transference of spirits. Evil forces transfer to those who use them or own them.

That is why it is so vital that we refuse to cooperate with any work of evil. We have to make a distinction between our old life of sin and our new life in Jesus Christ. I can't understand married Christians who keep pictures or love letters in their jewelry boxes or little keepsake boxes of their old boyfriends or girlfriends. They foolishly tie little ribbons around the collection while Satan is busy tying up their heart.

When we come into the born again experience, the Apostle Paul says, "Old things are passed away; behold all things are become new." You can't be truly free to enjoy the new until you make sure old things are passed away.

After we cleanse our hearts and purge our lives of evil influences, we must stay on guard. The devil is always willing to trip us up with something that will permit him access into our lives. We have to stay on guard by staying full of the Word of God and the Holy Spirit. The Holy Spirit can prompt us when we must get rid of something or change our association with someone.

In I Corinthians 2:12-14, Paul wrote, *"Now we have received, not the spirit of the world, but the Spirit who is from God, that we might know the things that have been freely given to us by God. These things we also speak, not in words which man's wisdom teaches but which the Holy Spirit teaches, comparing spiritual things with spiritual. But the natural man does not receive the things of the Spirit of God, for they are foolishness to him; nor can he know them, because they are spiritually discerned."* Here we are taught by Paul that there are two spirits: the spirit of the world, and the spirit of God. One or the other will control your mind and your decisions.

I cannot know the things of God unless I am yielded to the Spirit of God. If I am controlled by the spirit of the world, I will not know the things of God. Jesus told the disciples that they would have to "continue in my Word," if they wanted to be considered His disciples. Continuing in the Word will help a Christian cleanse his mind, his heart and his home from all corrupting influences. If a person is worldly minded, he may be controlled by greed, lust and power because those are the controlling forces in the world. That person cannot know the things of God.

Search the scriptures and earnestly ask the Holy Spirit to point out things in your possessions or your relationships that grieve Him. Things that are contrary to Biblical teachings will grieve the Holy Spirit. When you are full of the Holy Spirit, He will attack greed, envy, jealously, bitterness or anything else in you that is unlike Jesus. The scriptures will scour you clean and conform you to a new standard of living. The scriptures will free you from the spirit of the world.

The second way to stay on your guard against the wiles of the devil is to keep your godly relationships in unity. I heard one man say that he had a very good relationship with God, but it was God's people he just couldn't love. That just cannot be. If you love God, you will love what He loves. God loves His people. Staying in unity with other members of the body of Christ is a safety guard. I love my wife more today than I did the day I married her. We have a greater unity now than ever before. I see the value in her life. She is valuable to me. The devil can't tear us apart because we won't give him a chance to do it.

We never go to bed at night without telling each other, "I love you!" When we keep everything right between us, Satan has no power to destroy our relationship. We try to stay in unity at all times. This makes us a threat to Satan's kingdom. I can put 1,000 to flight, but when she joins me, together we can put 10,000 to flight. The devil knows that if the body of Christ ever gets over their prejudices we will win this battle.

God works in multiples. Satan works in divisions. We must give no place to the devil. Amos 3:3 asks, "Can two walk together, unless they are agreed?" Disagreements open the door for evil spirits to attack.

The spirit of this world is always trying to gain control of the child of God in order to pull him back into sin. We have to be vigilant to keep this from happening. It is time for Christians to stop being deceived and misled. Evil company corrupts good manners, morals and character. Garbage in— garbage out. Hang onto the world's system and spirits will attempt to transfer into your life. Instead, why not give yourself completely to the study and application of the Word of God to your life in obedience to the Holy Spirit? Then you will avoid the corrupting influences of the world, and enjoy the sweet communion of the Lord.

CHAPTER EIGHT:
THE POWER OF HEALTHY SOUL TIES

Wholeness or completeness is a place of peace in the inner being of a person. One who is complete does not walk around feeling like something is out of kilter. This person lives with a sense of balance and purpose in life. He or she is not constantly feeling diminished by others or by circumstances of life. Have you ever heard of someone who can "roll with the punches?" This person seems to come through bad times without losing his sense of wholeness.

During my decades of ministry, I have seen married couples who embody this sense of wholeness. They live together and even begin to act alike. What I am saying is that they are so knit together, although they don't look alike, they almost act and react like Siamese twins. They are so fully complete in each other it is hard to imagine the one without the other. At the same time, each is so fully complete in Christ that if they had to go on without the other partner, their Christian walk would not falter. A whole or complete person is one who has a healthy soul; whose mind, will and emotions are mature and balanced. This is the Lord's goal for every Christian.

The human soul is actually the part that brings balance between one's spirit and body and between oneself and others around him. Thus, the human soul is very often the target for satanic attacks. If the enemy can bring about imbalance in the area of the soul, the Christian may find himself being super- spiritual or extremely carnal. A healthy human soul helps the Christian live *"in the world, but not be of the world,"* as the Apostle Paul exhorted us to do. Some ministers ignore the importance of the soul, concentrating totally on the spiritual man. They believe that to minister on issues of the soul makes them somehow less spiritual. The problem with this sort of imbalance is the soul is the relational part of the Christian and needs as much attention as his spirit.

When a person becomes emotionally involved with another, often what is formed has come to be called a "soul-tie." This is the tie that binds together friendships, parent/child relationships as well as marriage relationships. Soul ties are a knitting together of minds, wills and emotions. Siblings can form soul ties. This is often and most easily observed in children born as multiples. Twins or triplets often have such a knitting together of their souls they can finish each other's sentences. Healthy soul ties can cause a person to feel richly fulfilled, happy and at peace.

In church circles today, the average Christian thinks soul ties are something to be avoided as being dangerous. They are not always bad. The scriptures give some examples of healthy soul ties and how they contributed to the success of God's plans. David was the youngest of his father's household who, to everyone's surprise was one day anointed king by the prophet Samuel. David was a ruddy, little fellow keeping sheep on the backside of his father's land while his stronger, more handsome brothers were doing great exploits in the service of their nation. David was the runt of the litter, but he had a heart of love for God that sent fragrant worship up into heaven. True worship always gets the Lord's attention.

David carried cheese and bread to his famous brothers one day while they were cowed down on the battlefield hiding from the Philistine champion, Goliath. In a whirlwind of faith and action, ruddy, little David busted the giant's head with a well-placed stone defeating the very foe the entire army of Israel had feared to face. David was hoisted upon the shoulders of rejoicing Israelites and carried to King Saul's tent.

Then, as David returned from the slaughter of the Philistine, Abner took him and brought him before Saul with the head of the Philistine in his hand. And Saul said to him, *"'Whose son are you, young man?' So David answered, 'I am the son of your servant Jesse, the Bethlehemite.'"* The story continues. *"Now when he had finished speaking to Saul, the soul of Jonathan was knit to the soul of David, and Jonathan loved him as his own soul. Saul took him that day, and would not let him go home to his father's house anymore. Then Jonathan and David made a covenant, because he loved him as his own soul"* (I Samuel 17:57, 18:1-3). Prince Jonathan, ruling heir to the throne and son of King Saul, formed a healthy soul tie with David that would continue into the next generation.

Godly soul ties are good. They should not be automatically avoided. The measure of a soul tie is this: does it bring you closer to the Lord? Does it cause you to feel peace within your own heart and in your relationship with Jesus Christ? I have known of ministers who have soul ties with young ministers. These young men form relationships with white-headed ministers who know how to teach, train and encourage. These are healthy and godly if they contribute to the work of God by moving the plan of God forward. God used the soul tie between David and Jonathan to bring about His plan of removing King Saul after King Saul disobeyed God's commands.

Perhaps King Solomon was remembering his father David's soul tie with his dear friend Jonathan when he wrote,

Two are better than one,

Because they have a good reward for their labor.

For if they fall, one will lift up his companion.

But woe to him who is alone when he falls,

For he has no one to help him up.

Again, if two lie down together, they will keep warm;

But how can one be warm alone?

Though one may be overpowered by another, two can withstand him.

And a threefold cord is not quickly broken (Ecclesiastes. 4:9-12).

This passage offers a perfect picture of a godly soul tie. Each party involved is more concerned about the other than himself. Notice how they are both concentrating their efforts on defeating the enemy, not each other. Healthy soul ties develop from a godly servant's heart.

King Solomon also wrote, A friend loves at all times (Proverbs 17:17a). This friend is in covenant relationship with you, determined to go the extra mile on your behalf. The little shepherd boy-turned-super-hero came into covenant relationship with Prince Jonathan. They loved each other with such devotion that what was important to the one was important to the other. Later, when King Saul grew madly jealous of David and plotted to kill him, Prince Jonathan orchestrated the plan to save David's life. When King Saul ruthlessly pursued David for years desiring to kill him, David refrained from retaliation even though he could have snuffed out King Saul's life one day. A friend loves at all times. God used this godly, covenant love between these two young men to save David's life and to reach into the next generation.

In another battle with the Philistines years later, Prince Jonathan and two of his brothers were killed while King Saul was wounded. After Saul understood there was no way of escape, he fell upon his own sword ending his life. David lamented the death of King Saul and his beloved friend Jonathan. His lamentation, the Song of the Bow, was taught to succeeding generations as a memorial. In the song David cried, I am distressed for you, my brother Jonathan; you have been very pleasant to me; your love to me was wonderful, surpassing the love of women (II Samuel. 1:26).

The love and devotion David and Jonathan had for each other is a testimony to the power of godly soul ties. Consider what David and Jonathan did. Jonathan was so tied to David he gave up the right to sit on the throne in order to defer to his friend, David. Jonathan was the natural heir, but he surrendered that. How many people do you know who for a friend would give up their right to be heir to the throne? Most people might give up something that doesn't matter or doesn't really cost them anything. David and Jonathan were so knit together they would give up anything for one another.

Years later, this covenant love was still strong in David's heart. He had finally been crowned king, and had made many conquests. Now David said, *"Is there still anyone who is left of the house of Saul, that I may show him kindness for Jonathan's sake?"* (II Samuel. 9:1). How amazing is that? For Jonathan's sake, David was willing to show favor to anyone left who descended from Jonathan's father; the same man who plotted David's death and hunted him like a dog for many years. Much to David's delight he discovered that not only was there a male descendant of Saul's still alive, but that this man was a son of his beloved friend, Jonathan. Mephibosheth was lame in his feet as a result of his nurse dropping him in her haste to hide him from those who wanted to kill all descendants of Saul. Yet, as a grown man, he and his family were brought to Jerusalem where he ate at the king's table for the rest of his life. A friend loves at all times. Jonathan's covenant of love saved David's life, moving forward the plan of God for Israel. Years later, even though his friend was dead, David carried the covenant of love into the next generation.

David probably knew something about covenant love and godly soul ties even before he met his dear friend Jonathan.

David would have learned as a young boy the oral tradition of his family, and how his father's birth had taken place as a result of healthy, godly soul ties a few generations earlier.

In the days when the judges ruled, long before King Saul was born, the land of Israel suffered a famine. Elimelech, a Bethlehemite, moved his family into the land of Moab in order to find work. Elimelech, his two sons and his wife, Naomi lived there about ten years. During this period of time Elimelech died and Naomi was left with her two sons, who had married women of Moab. One was Orpah, and the other was Ruth. Then both sons, Mahlon and Chilion also died. After their deaths, Naomi decided to return to the land of Israel because the famine was over, and she had no reason to remain in that foreign, heathen land.

Here is where we see a perfect example of godly soul ties which God used to accomplish His purpose for Israel's future. Naomi kissed Orpah and Ruth and bid them to return to their mother's house. The two girls cried and cried for they truly loved Naomi. She must have been a wonderful mother-in-law. Orpah went back to her mother's house, but Ruth clung to Naomi. *"And she said, 'Look, your sister-in-law has gone back to her people and to her gods; return after your sister-in-law.' But Ruth said: "Entreat me not to leave you, or to turn back from following after you; for wherever you go, I will go; and wherever you lodge, I will lodge; your people shall be my people, and your God, my God. Where you die, I will die, and there will I be buried. The LORD do so to me, and more also, if anything but death parts you and me"* (Ruth 1:15-17). Her soul tie with Naomi was so strong she was willing to part with her own land and people in order to stay with her mother-in-law. Some Christians have asked the question, "Can you have a healthy soul tie with a family member?" Here is the answer. Naomi and Ruth shared a bond of love within their family relationship.

Perhaps these two women had spent long hours working together, interacting with each other and sharing each other's sorrows and burdens. Through this intimate sharing, their souls became knit together. They understood and valued each other. A healthy soul tie was formed. Notice how Naomi did not use her bond of love with the girls to force them to leave their land and people in order to travel with her to Israel. How frightening it must have been for an older woman to consider the journey alone, yet she did not try to manipulate them into going with her. In fact, she tried to get them to remain among their own people. Ruth responded with words and actions that made it clear, "Because of this bond of love between us, you are my people."

Naomi realized Ruth would not be sent back, so she moved her from her legal place of daughter-in-law, to a soul and spirit place of daughter. *"There was a relative of Naomi's husband, a man of great wealth, of the family of Elimelech. His name was Boaz. So Ruth the Moabitess said to Naomi, 'Please let me go to the field, and glean heads of grain after him in whose sight I may find favor.' And she said to her, 'Go, my daughter'"* (Ruth 2:1-2).

Naomi continued to manifest her covenant of love with Ruth by deciding to provide for her just as a mother would for her daughter. *"Then Naomi her mother-in-law said to her, 'My daughter, shall I not seek security for you that it may be well with you? Now Boaz, whose young women you were with, is he not our relative? In fact, he is winnowing barley tonight at the threshing floor'"* (Ruth 3:1-2). Naomi knew the local customs of her people. She operated within those customs to try and secure a husband for Ruth.

Several things happen when people have healthy soul ties. People become very protective of each other. Men become protective of their wives and children. I am very protective of my wife and will readily defend her. If you insult my children or grandchildren, I will feel very emotional about that. You might say something against me, but I cannot tolerate it if you attack my wife or kids. That's why Satan hates healthy soul ties. He hates the unity it produces. When you have a wholesome soul tie you will always have unity.

Soul ties, which exist between family members, can be extremely strong. The reason for this is that it falls into the divine order of God. Healthy soul ties were God's way of assuring the health and welfare of the family unit. Healthy soul ties cause families to want to provide for each other and to protect each other.

When I was a pastor in New Orleans, I was preaching one Sunday morning and noticed a young, teenaged girl slip into the back of the auditorium. She seemed to be hanging on every word of my sermon. I could see the spiritual hunger written on her face. After the service, I tried to make it back to the doors to speak with her, but she slipped out and was gone. My heart ached for her.

The following Wednesday evening she returned. When the invitation to be born again was given, she responded accepting Jesus Christ into her heart. I spoke to her for a few minutes and discovered her name was Cindy. She seemed reluctant to give any more personal information, so I didn't push her. The next Sunday morning Cindy was there again; this time with a young girl about the age of ten. After service Cindy came to me with her sister asking, "Brother Gorman, would you put Jesus in my little sister's heart too?" I prayed with Cindy and Debbie. They raced out with a look of joy on their faces.

During the week, I couldn't get their little faces out of my mind. I prayed that the Lord would bless them and keep them. I was thrilled the next Sunday morning that they were there again and this time they had a little boy with them who looked to be about five years old. Again when the salvation call was made they came forward with little Johnny in tow and asked me to "put Jesus in his heart." The next week they were all three there with radiant faces obviously enjoying their new-found faith in Jesus Christ.

I spoke with Cindy following the service telling her some of the ladies would like to visit during the week so they could meet their parents. Cindy dropped her head and said she didn't want anyone to visit because her mother was a prostitute. The next week I greeted Cindy as she came into the church. I reached out to touch her arm, but she could barely hide the grimace of pain. "Is there anything wrong?" I asked. The young teen looked at the floor and responded, "Oh, nothing." I asked my wife and another lady to take her to the ladies' room and see if there might be something wrong with her back or her arm. My wife, Virginia, returned with tears in her eyes, telling me the child had been so badly beaten her undergarments were sticking to her skin.

Anger rose in me like a volcano. I told Cindy we would hire an attorney and immediately begin proceedings to find a new home for her and her siblings. She began to cry saying, "Oh Brother Gorman, if you do that who will take care of my mother and pray for her? Who will show her how much she needs Jesus?" She was willing to endure the dangers of her own home in order that her mother could be saved. Soul ties cause people to provide for and protect each other.

The fledgling church in Acts was willing to endure all sorts of hardships for each other. They were powerful because they had healthy soul ties. *"Now the multitude of those who believed were of one heart and one soul; neither did anyone say that any of the things he possessed was his own, but they had all things in common"* (Acts 4:32). The Word of God records this healthy soul tie. Now look at what those healthy soul ties produced. *"And with great power the apostles gave witness to the resurrection of the Lord Jesus. And great grace was upon them all"* (Acts 4:33). Healthy soul ties produced a healthy church filled with the power to witness the resurrection of the Lord Jesus!

This is why healthy soul ties are dangerous to the enemy. He wants to destroy the unity of both the church and the family. Rebellion in the family exists because there are no healthy soul ties. The dad jumps up and leaves at will. He doesn't care if his children have food or not. The mom runs off with another guy and leaves the children looking out the window wondering if she's ever coming back. Families are devastated when there is no strong commitment for the welfare of the others. Nature's way is to say, "What's mine is mine!" In the marriage ceremony you are supposed to be pledging, "What is mine is now yours."

My wife was a young widow when I met her. She knows what it is like to grieve over the accidental death of a young husband, drive herself to the hospital to give birth, and provide for her baby with no companion to help. When we married, she thought what was mine was ours and what was hers was hers! As we grew in the Lord and in relationship with each other, healthy soul ties were created which developed a bond of trust and appreciation. Now, what's ours is hers and hers is ours. I leave her to manage our checkbook for the benefit of the whole family because a healthy soul tie developed between us.

Healthy soul ties can be created between friends, siblings and church members, but the strongest soul tie between humans should be between the husband and wife. *"So husbands ought to love their own wives as their own bodies; he who loves his wife loves himself. For no one ever hated his own flesh, but nourishes and cherishes it, just as the Lord does the church. For we are members of His body, of His flesh and of His bones. For this reason a man shall leave his father and mother and be joined to his wife, and the two shall become one flesh"* (Eph. 5:28-31). A spiritual principle you must understand is that *"One can put a thousand to flight and two can put ten thousand to flight."* Satan knows that unity in the Children of God brings the blessings of God including God releasing angelic beings to come to our aid. It starts with the bond between husbands and wives.

I once knew a Christian brother who had morning sickness every time his wife was pregnant. He vomited every morning. Sometimes he was five or six hundred miles away for a meeting, yet he would have to get out of bed and throw up. Whenever she got sick, he got sick. Adam explained this in Genesis 2:23 when he said, *"This is now bone of my bones and flesh of my flesh; she shall be called Woman, because she was taken out of Man."* This Christian man was so bonded to his wife that he felt in his own body some of the things she was feeling.

The next verse in Genesis explains why the marriage vows are so sacred in the eyes of God. *"Therefore, a man shall leave his father and mother and be joined to his wife, and they shall become one flesh"* (Verse 24). The marital bond causes the couple to become joined or glued together. Have you ever glued something together? If you try to pull it apart, it is much more than the glue that is damaged.

Many Americans today view marriage as a legal contract. The paper is the glue that holds them together. They think if they suddenly fall out of love, they can just tear up the paper and that is the only thing that gets torn. Instead, the marriage is like gluing two pieces of wood together. If you pull them apart, the wood itself is torn and damaged. That is why divorce is so shattering.

In fact, often soul ties created in marriage because of sexual intercourse are even stronger than two pieces of wood being glued together. Sexual intercourse makes you one with the other person. That makes soul ties created through sexual intercourse, but later broken, like me taking my wife's arm and pulling on her, while someone else holds her other arm and we try to tear her arms off her shoulders. When you become one like this you would have to be torn apart. It's not just a piece of paper which is being torn. That's why divorce is so devastating. It not only affects the husband and wife, but the children too. A shameful fact is that over half the children raised in American churches are being torn apart by divorce. It shouldn't be so. Creating and maintaining healthy soul ties will prevent this from happening.

Divorced families today have to be emotionally healed in the same way they would have to be physically healed if their bodies were torn apart in some car accident. Without exception, divorce can be so destructive it tears people apart leaving such deep emotional hurts that some never learn how to be healed. They become bitter and resentful instead of becoming healed and whole.

The Book of Acts tells us there was such a bond of soul ties in the early church that, if these people sold property, they came and laid it at the disciples' feet in order for the disciples to distribute it to help the needy. They didn't bring their finances in order to manipulate or gain power over people. They realized the Lord had provided it for them in order to make a difference in the lives of others. No one man claimed this to be theirs. They held all things in common.

I believe it is possible that, before Jesus returns, the churches will come back to that. It appears that we can't have caring, trusting unity without some kind of crisis bringing us to that place. During the Great Depression, whatever a neighbor had belonged to all. My mother told me that neighbors planted large gardens with peas, turnips, corn and other vegetables. Everyone shared with others. One neighbor shared his squash, the other shared his green beans and another brought his potatoes to be distributed for the benefit of the neighborhood.

Why do I say it is going to come back to that? The average Christian still says, "That's mine! I'll let you have it if you sign right here." Satan keeps the church divided and ineffective with this mentality because it often produces feelings of envy. The scriptures tell us, *"For where envy and self-seeking exist, confusion and every evil thing are there"* (James 3:16). There is coming a time when our financial status and social conditions will change. If you knew you were going to go to some lady's house to eat red beans and rice because your pantry was empty, you would treat her nice because you need her. Jesus prayed that we would become one. When that prayer is answered, we will devastate the devil.

When a family is one, they are not bickering and back-biting. They hold all possessions in the common interest. We get caught up in what is ours, but when we begin to prefer our brother, unity is created which cannot be broken. I see the church in the end time becoming so unified with each other that it will break the strongholds of Satan, and literally bind principalities and powers. Then the glory will come down stamping out evil and causing righteousness to prevail.

Wholesome soul ties can be good for the individual, the marriage, the family and the church. How can you know what constitutes a healthy soul tie? Your greatest protection is when you have a soul tie with the Lord Jesus Christ. *"But he who is joined to the Lord is one spirit with Him"* (I Corinthians

6:17). The Apostle Paul was teaching the church that the body was not for sexual immorality, but for the Lord. He counseled them to break off sexually immoral conduct. He told them to consider that joining themselves to harlots was like taking Jesus himself and joining him to a harlot. Paul said, *"Or do you not know that he who is joined to a harlot is one body with her? For the two, He says, shall become one flesh"* (I Corinthians 6:16). He taught them to consider themselves one with the Lord Jesus in the same way the husband and wife are one.

He counseled them to have the mind of Christ. "Think about things the way Jesus thinks about them," he was saying to the church. Our mind, will and emotions should be so tied to Christ Jesus that we think like Him. We should be determined to let nothing enter in that does not line up with His thinking. We must cleave to our Lord, be glued to, be knitted to Him in a soul and spirit tie that cannot be broken.

Once a healthy soul tie is established with the Lord, it is easy to evaluate soul ties by the Word of God to see if they are healthy or not. Submit your relationships to the test of the scriptures. If your relationships are producing peace, joy and love, they are healthy and wholesome. If your relationships cause conflict and confusion in your mind and heart, you will probably find unhealthy soul ties. Remember that not every person who is friendly to you can necessarily be your friend. Jonathan and David were both in a place where they could create and maintain a healthy soul tie which continued even after death. The love they had for each other caused them to be better men and better servants of the Lord.

A healthy soul tie is fertile ground. It leaves room for you to grow and mature without condemning you for your mistakes. A healthy soul tie causes those involved to receive love from each other without jealousy or suspicion. It does not clamor for more than one can give. Wholesome soul ties feel safe and protective. You never have to worry about being uncovered or belittled in front of others.

The scriptures offer examples of healthy soul ties as well as examples of unhealthy soul ties. This gives Christians the opportunity to evaluate their relationships in the light of the Word of God. Since natural tendencies pull us into soul ties, Satan is not ignorant of this fact. He likes to tempt us with something that is normal or natural. However, he never leaves it in the realm of normal or natural. He wrests and twists it to pervert it and make it something it was never meant to be. That's the reason soul ties should be carefully formed within the boundaries of the scriptures.

Before you plunge into a deep relationship with someone, seek the heart of God. Evaluate whether or not this person is likely to be able to keep the relationship in line with godly character. If not, be very hesitant to open your mind, will and emotions to this person. Be careful that you do not share your heart with this person, and later discover that they are incapable of maintaining a healthy soul tie that glorifies God. If you always keep foremost in your mind your desire to exalt God in all things, you will be successful in your relationships. Healthy soul ties will create stronger marriages, families and churches. Healthy soul ties will cause a person to feel at peace while walking in a balanced sense of purpose and acceptance. This is the will of God for His people.

CHAPTER NINE:
THE DANGEROUS POWER OF UNGODLY SOUL TIES

Although soul ties can be healthy, producing many benefits for Christians as well as the Kingdom of God, we must also recognize there are unhealthy soul ties which bind Christians and keep them from peace and balance. These soul ties must be broken before they will ever achieve anything significant in their faith walk. Wrong and unhealthy soul ties bind and destroy.

Soul ties should only be formed between those who have as their absolute foundation a strong and vibrant relationship with Jesus Christ. Jesus is called the chief cornerstone for a reason. No foundation can properly be laid without a chief cornerstone. The cornerstone of any successful marriage or friendship must be Jesus Christ. Peter quoted, *"Therefore, it is also contained in the Scripture, 'Behold, I lay in Zion a chief cornerstone, elect, precious, and he who believes on Him will by no means be put to shame.' Therefore, to you who believe, He is precious; but to those who are disobedient, 'The stone which the builders rejected' has become the chief cornerstone"* (I Peter 2:6-7). Peter was quoting Jesus whom Matthew recorded as making this declaration in Matthew 21:42. Jesus was quoting Isaiah 28:16. Isaiah was quoting Psalm 118:22-23. This valuable truth was passed by King David to the prophet Isaiah who handed it to Jesus who then handed it to Peter. Peter called the Lord's cornerstone *"precious."* Have you ever had something precious handed to you that had been in your family for generations upon generations? That is what came into Peter's hands and heart that day — "elect, precious and he who believes on Him will by no means be put to shame."

This chief cornerstone, Jesus Christ, is the only foundation upon which a person may safely build any relationship. Natural relationships such as those found in marriages, parent/child relationships and friendships are prone to become twisted and imbalanced if the foundation does not include the Chief Cornerstone. Soul ties formed between persons who equally share the goal of bringing glory and honor to Jesus Christ will be able to overcome any force brought to bear against it.

Unhealthy soul ties formed without Jesus Christ as the Chief Cornerstone most often result in one or both parties being harmed or destroyed. Samson is a prime example of one who formed an unhealthy soul tie. This dangerous soul tie finally reduced him to nothing, and ultimately brought about his death. His foundation was not a desire to serve and please the Lord God, but his desire was to fulfill his own pleasures.

Samson had been born for a godly purpose. He was equipped with incredible power, but somehow he left his teaching and training and became sexually involved with an immoral woman. His soul became so tied to her that he gave away the sacred secret of his immense strength. Samson's death proved one cannot fulfill the purposes of God, and make love to the world at the same time. It is true he killed more enemies on the day of his death than throughout his whole life, but God's design for him was more than that. Before he was even born, God told his parents this child would *begin to deliver Israel from the hand of the Philistines.*

Sadly, the beginning of Israel's deliverance was cut short by a soul tie which bound and blinded Samson and destroyed his promise.

How many men and women of God have you known who formed unhealthy soul ties that destroyed their ministry? It happened to me. It has only been by tearful and sincere repentance, as well as submission to the Lord and the church that I have been restored. When my sin was uncovered in 1986, I lost everything except what was most precious to me. By the grace of God I was blessed to keep my wife and children, my relationship with the Lord and my deep-seated desire to love and serve Him. I held tightly to the foundation that had been so dear to me; the Chief Cornerstone was my Rock of Ages. By His grace I came through and continued my pulpit ministry. Eventually, I was re-instated with the Assemblies of God denomination. Unfortunately, that is not the common end of the story for most individuals who make the mistake of forming unwholesome soul ties.

Women can often be more susceptible to forming ungodly soul ties when they look for the wrong things in a man in order to make them feel loved and accepted. I have ministered to countless women who formed soul ties with truly bad men. Their decision not only ruined their lives, but the lives of their children as well. These are the women who mistakenly believed their love would somehow change the minds and hearts of those worldly men. The truth is-- the only love that will change any mind and heart is the love of Jesus Christ being fully and completely received by that individual.

John 3:16 says, *"For God so loved the world that He gave His only begotten Son, that whoever believes in Him should not perish but have everlasting life."* Yes, God loved the world, but that was not enough. That was only part of the equation. The other part was that the members of this world whom He loved had to respond by believing in Him, accepting Him, trusting Him and fully relying upon Him. James tells us that it is not enough to believe that there is one God. *"You believe that there is one God. You do well. Even the demons believe — and tremble! But do you want to know, O foolish man, that faith without works is dead?"* (James 2:19-20). True belief in God will move one to trust in Him, submit to Him and fully rely upon Him. This is the only way a person can truly change.

This cannot be accomplished by the woman saying, "Well, my man knows God loves him because I show him that godly love. That's enough for me." The truth is that will not be enough for him. He must know and experience the Lord Jesus Christ as his Savior. He must submit his life to be founded on Christ before any healthy soul tie can ever be created and maintained. Women fall into an ungodly belief that somehow their power can change a human heart. These women are often shipwrecked on the shores of disillusionment.

Some of the most powerful soul ties are formed by sexual relations. Engaging in sexual intercourse is like opening the window to your soul. You become linked to that person in more ways than just the physical act of sexual relations. One youth minister uses the example of the rose to demonstrate to teen girls the damage done by multiple sex partners. He gives a beautiful rose to a teen on the front row and asks her to peel off a petal then hand the rose to the next girl. By the time this beautiful flower has been passed around the room, there is nothing left but an ugly stem and sharp thorns. The Apostle Paul had to deal with this truth when he taught the church at Corinth. A group of Corinthians had embraced the gospel of Jesus Christ, but made the classic mistake of simply adding Jesus to their lives instead of turning their lives over to Him for a complete change.

Paul encouraged believers at Corinth not to keep company with anyone named a brother who is "sexually immoral, or covetous, or an idolater, or a reviler, or a drunkard, or an extortioner-- not even to eat with this person." He precedes this direction by saying that he was not talking about people in the world, but people in the church who claim Jesus Christ, but continue on with their sinful lives. He teaches that we are not to be judging those on the outside, meaning the world, because God has already judged them as sinful. But we are to judge those on the inside; in other words, we are to evaluate their behaviors. If they are not changing their behavior in accordance with their professed faith in Jesus Christ, we are to leave off fellowship with that person.

He addressed those who are sexually immoral. Then he taught; *"Now the body is not for sexual immorality but for the Lord, and the Lord for the body."* He asked the congregation, *"Do you not know that your bodies are members of Christ? Shall I then take the members of Christ and make them members of a harlot? Certainly not! Or do you not know that he who is joined to a harlot is one body with her? For the two, He says, shall become one flesh?*

But he who is joined to the Lord is one spirit with Him. Flee sexual immorality" (I Corinthians 6:15-18a).

"He who is joined to the Lord is one spirit with Him," wrote Paul. The prophet Amos wrote years earlier, *"Can two walk together unless they are agreed?"* If your spirit is truly joined with the Lord, you must not allow anything to cause a disagreement between you and the Spirit of Christ in you. Many a woman in her haste to get a man has submitted her body and spirit to him through intercourse even though he was unsaved. What happened? Suddenly there was a disagreement in her spirit. The Spirit of Christ in her cannot agree with the spirit of the devil in that man. She should expect a lot of conflict.

You cannot change a man by submitting your godly spirit to him in the hopes of winning over his ungodly spirit. This is wrong and dangerous thinking. If you are truly in love with Jesus Christ, but think you love this man, wait until his spirit has been transformed by a true, born again experience with Jesus before you join yourself to him in holy matrimony and in sexual intimacy. Otherwise, crisis after crisis and tragedy after tragedy will be your lot in life. Two cannot walk together except they are agreed. Your spirit cannot be joined to a spirit that is not of Christ Jesus. If you make this mistake, you are opening wide to terrible confusion in your soul.

Soul ties are ties that bind mind, will and emotions to another person. If you are going to bind your mind to another, you must be sure you are like-minded. If you are going to bind your will to another you must be sure you will the same things in life. If his will is for drugs and alcohol, yet your will is for a safe home and healthy children, you've got a problem. If you are going to bind your emotions to another, you must make sure that he is emotionally sound. If he is ruled by base and intemperate passions, your emotions can expect an unholy roller coaster ride.

Unhealthy soul ties are the reason people came under the power of corrupt leaders like Hitler, Jim Jones and David Koresh. These men were masters at causing people to open their minds to their control. God has never called us to open our minds to someone else's control. He has called us to carefully think through and examine teachings in order to discover the truth for ourselves. Luke, the author of the book of Acts, commended the Bereans, *"These were more fair-minded than those in Thessalonica, in that they received the word with all readiness, and searched the Scriptures daily to find out whether these things were so"* (Acts 17:11).

Corrupt leaders convince their followers to vacate their minds in order to enter into a passive state where deceptive thoughts can be planted. Then these controlling, manipulative leaders berate and condemn their followers if they evaluate and examine the messages they impart. Ungodly soul ties are formed through intellectually suppressing others. Luke, the disciple of Paul and his constant traveling companion, did not at all agree with this approach. He was impressed with the people of Berea who took the time to listen to Paul's teaching, and then evaluate those thoughts according to the Holy Scriptures. The truth of Jesus Christ invites examination and is not afraid of it. The truth stands the test of time and the test of honest inquiry.

Not only do corrupt leaders attempt to use mind control to form ungodly soul ties, but they often seek to control their followers by perverted sex. The joining of one body to another produces a soul tie that can easily be twisted and perverted. The story of Jacob's daughter offers a vivid picture of this truth.

"Now Dinah the daughter of Leah, whom she had borne to Jacob, went out to see the daughters of the land. And when Shechem the son of Hamor the Hivite, prince of the country saw her he took her and lay with her and violated her. His soul was strongly attracted to Dinah the daughter of Jacob and he loved the young woman and spoke kindly to the young woman. So Shechem spoke to his father Hamor, saying, 'Get me this young woman as a wife.' And Jacob heard that he had defiled Dinah his daughter. Now his sons were with his livestock in the field so Jacob held his peace until they came. Then Hamor, the father of Shechem, went out to Jacob to speak with him. And the sons of Jacob came in from the field when they heard it and the men were grieved and very angry because he had done a disgraceful thing in Israel by lying with Jacob's daughter, a thing which ought not to be done. But Hamor spoke with them saying, 'The soul of my son Shechem longs for your daughter. Please give her to him as a wife'" (Genesis 34:1-8).

In plain terms, Dinah, daughter of Jacob and Leah, was raped by Prince Shechem. He saw her, he lusted after her and he raped her. Afterwards the scripture records that "his soul was strongly attracted to her." His mind, will and emotions were bound to her. Notice that it doesn't say she was bound to him. He became bound to her. It was not her fault. Her beauty did not invite rape. His lust prompted the rape. His desire to steal and then control was the motivation for this evil act. Irregardless, an unwholesome soul tie was formed. Shechem did not want to live without Dinah. He told his father what he wanted in no uncertain terms. He did not intend to be denied. He intended to have Dinah, and she would have no say about the matter.

Have you ever wondered how men, and even some women, can begin stalking another person? I have ministered to women who finally gathered the courage to leave an abusive husband or boyfriend only to be stalked and threatened by them. The same was the case with this evil prince. A soul tie was formed in Shechem when he violated Dinah. He did not intend to let her go. Notice how after his cruel and heartless violation of her, he "loved the young woman and spoke kindly to her." That is not love! That is what he called love. Love does not rape and then afterward speak kindly. What did he say? "I'm sorry for doing that, but now I love you and will not let you go back to your father's house?" That is a sick and sorry excuse for love. Some women get confused by those words. The man violates her, and then speaks kindly, lacing his speech with words of love. Confusion sets into her heart. "Perhaps he does love me. Maybe I deserved that. I guess I have no choice now, but to stay with him." The woman gets sick and twisted in her mind because her mind has become joined with his sick and twisted mind. A soul tie was established. It wasn't her fault. She was the victim. She was raped, but still a soul tie was formed and confusion entered her mind. That unhealthy soul tie must be broken. That confused mind has to be transformed by the truth of the Word of God.

Perverted sexual relationships establish unhealthy soul ties that can destroy body, soul and spirit. Paul dealt with this in Corinth because it was a common practice of the Corinthians to worship in temples by using both male and female prostitutes. The false gods of Corinth supposedly gave power through these prostitutes to give special favors and answered prayers through lascivious acts of sex. This was a common practice in the community. It still is today in many areas of the world.

An ancient practice in India includes sex slaves as young as five, both male and female, being sold by their parents to the temple for the use and abuse of worshippers. Paul confronted this practice and expressly forbade it among believers. "Do not be joined to a harlot," he commanded the Greeks. This perverted sex opened the participant up to all manner of evil spirits. As hard as it is to believe, Paul had to confront another manifestation of perverted sex when he told the church to excommunicate one among them who refused to stop sleeping with his father's wife. He instructed them to "deliver such a one to Satan for the destruction of the flesh that his spirit may be saved in the day of the Lord Jesus Christ." This perverted sexual practice opened the door for this man to reap destruction in his body. Paul hoped the man would be chastened enough to repent and turn from his wickedness.

Paul's advice achieved its intended goal because in II Corinthians 2:6-8, he encouraged the church to receive the repentant man back into fellowship and *"reaffirm your love to him."* The man had decided to fully believe in, rely on and trust in Jesus Christ. He left his sinful behavior. He broke off his soul ties with his step-mother and stopped his incestuous relations. Because of his repentance and obvious actions to change his life, he was received into fellowship again.

His was an example of parental soul ties being sordidly perverted. Paul brought order to this man's life saving him from the punishment of hell. Soul ties between parents and children can be healthy and valuable in society, and in the Kingdom of God. On the other hand, these soul ties can be twisted and perverted to become damaging, unwholesome and downright criminal. Behind closed doors of many households today there are scenes of unrighteous soul ties and evil sexual practices. Fathers take their daughters to bed and grossly violate them. Brothers creep into their sister's room at night and vilely commit sexual crimes. In some households, fathers and sons engage in this horrible crime together, leaving shattered and broken pieces of a little girl behind. As hard as it may be to believe, there are even mothers who commit unspeakable acts of perverted sex against their children. These are examples of soul ties twisted and abused for the momentary pleasure of the perpetrator.

Parents can also have unhealthy soul ties with their children which do not involve sexual crimes. These parents cater to the child's every need, making sure the child has a clear understanding that she is the princess and the parents are there to fulfill her every wish. Some Christian parents make the mistake of believing that by serving in such a self-sacrificing manner, the child is being taught how to be a servant. Instead, the child is being taught how to be served. That same child may grow up incapable of fulfilling her marriage vows because she was never taught how to serve someone else's needs. She was only taught how to have her needs fulfilled. Have you ever heard of someone needing to cut the apron strings? That saying was coined to describe this situation. Today we have grown men in their 30's and 40's still living in their parents' basement because they were never required to grow up. Mommy is still trotting downstairs to ask him what he wants to eat for breakfast. It is a nauseating shame.

Children are often getting married and returning with their spouses to live in their parents' home. This is a dangerous manifestation of unhealthy soul ties. Some people argue that it is a way to save up money for a house or apartment, but I say you should save that money before you decide to marry a wife. If you aren't responsible enough to have your own place, are you going to be responsible enough to provide for your wife? Often finances are used to disguise the fact that a child has no intention of leaving the unhealthy soul tie he or she has formed with the parents.

God made the order of this matter very clear in Genesis 2:24, *"Therefore a man shall leave his father and mother and be joined to his wife, and they shall become one flesh."* The scripture is very clear: men should leave, cleave and be joined. Leave your soul ties with your parents. Cleave to your wife. Join yourself to her by forming a healthy soul tie with her. Cut the apron strings to mama or that soul tie will come back to strangle the relationship you think you have with your wife.

There is another kind of damaging soul tie I would like you to consider. This soul tie is created by people who are given to flatteries. They use flattery to establish themselves in the minds and emotions of others in such a way others become dependent upon the flatterer for their sense of self-worth. People who cannot leave church until the pastor "glad-hands" them are open to control because of these flatteries. There are many pastors who love to use flattery to control and manipulate their members. They lavish praise on someone for their beautiful voice, but it is only an attempt to make sure the member continues to bring big offerings into the church coffers.

"A lying tongue hates those who are crushed by it, and a flattering mouth works ruin" (Proverbs 26:28). The Amplified Bible states, *"A lying tongue hates those it wounds and crushes, and a flattering mouth works ruin."* Watch out for flatteries. Flattery by its very definition is insincere and excessive praise. Flatteries often are the result of that person needing to overcompensate for the fact he secretly chewed you to pieces with lying words earlier in the week. Flatteries open the mind, will and emotions to control and manipulation. Remember the key to understanding the difference between a compliment and flattery is sincerity.

I am always suspicious of flatteries. I do not open my soul to them because they are dangerously used to manipulate and control. Flatteries can be used to manipulate others into becoming anxious to please. Flattery can establish unhealthy soul ties because it exploits one person's desire to be accepted and approved. Everyone has a desire to be accepted and approved, but the flatterer seeks to exploit this need in a person and seeks to gain power over him. Guard yourself against flatteries. Brothers and sisters in Christ may offer you sincere compliments from time to time. Those should be graciously received, but if it tends to become flattery, avoid being controlled and manipulated by it. Don't let this strategy of the enemy form an unhealthy soul tie in you.

American Christians today are concerned with their emotional well-being, often much more than other brothers and sisters around the world. The fact is that many Americans have time to be more indulgent about their emotional health because they are not consumed with just trying to earn bread for the day like so many others in developing or third world countries. Because of this, Christians are flocking to counseling sessions, but there is a danger in this. Non-Christian counseling can be a snare used to establish ungodly soul ties.

Remember a soul tie is a binding of the mind, will and emotions. Letting an ungodly counselor get a hold of your mind, will and emotions can result in some wrong thinking. If you are a born-again believer, yet are still struggling with emotional issues that seem beyond your control, seek the help of a godly Christian counselor. I have been counseling for decades and have seen first- hand the dangers that exist when a person opens his soul to the wrong counselor. Remember the soul is the connecting point between the person's body and spirit. How can you be open in your mind, will and emotions to another person's thoughts if their thoughts are produced on the basis of their sinful life still ruled by the devil? You have nothing in common with the world, or the counselors of the world. Break off these ungodly alliances. Instead, seek a Christian counselor who will lead and guide you by the Word of God.

If you are feeling prompted now by the Holy Spirit to examine your relationships with others, be quick to do it. Ask the Holy Spirit to reveal to you any ungodly soul ties. Then take them to Jesus in a spirit of repentance. It is very likely you did not mean to form these soul ties. Perhaps they were formed in you while you were very young and until now you have never examined them. Ask yourself, "Does this relationship bring glory to God? Would I be glad to have Jesus right in the middle of our relationship or would I be ashamed?" If those questions bother you, take time to repent. Jesus wants you to have healthy relationships based on honor and respect for Him first, and then for the other person. If that cannot be done, you may very well need to part with this person altogether. Unwholesome soul ties can prevent you from developing and maintaining a healthy relationship with Jesus Christ.

Desire above everything that your relationships glorify God and move the plan of God forward. David and Jonathan modeled this for us. Naomi and Ruth also modeled this for us. Jesus Himself modeled this for us when He prayed that we would become one with the Father. The New Testament church members of Acts accepted that model and were of one heart and one soul, joined to the Lord and one with His purposes. Your greatest defense against ungodly soul ties is to maintain the strongest possible soul tie with your Heavenly Father.

Soul ties that produce life and peace in the Holy Ghost should be enjoyed. However, if your peace and emotional well-being is being wrongly affected by someone, take the time to examine whether or not an unhealthy soul tie has been formed. If so, hurry to cut it off so you can be one mind and one spirit with the Lord Jesus Christ. Jesus said, *"You shall love the Lord your God with all your heart, and with all your soul, and with your entire mind"* (Matthew 22:37). Everything that attempts to pull you away from this sort of soul tie must be rejected.

CHAPTER TEN:
THE TRUTH ABOUT GENERATIONAL CURSES

Is there such a thing as generational curses? Churches around the world debate the subject while church members continue to struggle with some of the same things their parents, grandparents and ancestors did. Call it whatever you want to, but what do we do with the struggles that exist in the lives of Christians that seem all too familiar to their family history? It is true Jesus became a curse for us in order to break all curses. It is also true that He came to die that all might be saved. Yet, not all are saved and not all are free from curses.

I know this is controversial, but we need to examine a Biblical truth. In Exodus 20:5, God commanded, *"You shall not bow down to them nor serve them. For I, the LORD your God, am a jealous God, visiting the iniquity of the fathers upon the children to the third and fourth generations of those who hate Me."* Rebellious and unrepentant sinners who hate God open the door for their children as well as successive generations to live under what may be rightfully called a generational curse.

There may be things in your family history which left the door open for Satan to attack you in a specific way. Have you ever been to a medical doctor who asked if your mother was still living, whether your daddy or anyone closely related had died and if so, of what? The doctor questions your family's medical history because he understands there is such a thing as inherited diseases or tendencies for these diseases. If your father died of a heart attack, the doctor will consider you at risk for a heart attack. If your mother suffered from diabetes, the doctor will probably run tests and search for this in your body.

Now consider this same line of thinking in relation to spiritual issues. Have you ever witnessed generations of God-haters? The father mocked God, hated God and died hating God. The next thing you know his son and grandson are spewing out the same kind of venom. Ever wondered why there are generations of alcoholics, drug abusers, wife abusers and child abusers? The curse, the authorization for sin that was particular to the father, got passed down to the son.

In Exodus, God told the children of Israel a curse like this can pass down, or *"be visited"* upon the fourth generation. The father may live long enough to watch his great-grandson grow up to be a God-cursing, God-hating, rebel just like himself. Ham, Noah's perverted son lived this long. Ham begot Cush, Cush begot Nimrod, and Nimrod built the tower of Babel. Nimrod was as much a God-hating rebel as his grandfather was. He entered into his grandfather's curse.

What is a curse anyway? Simply said, a curse is special permission for the devil to attack in a special manner. A curse may be sent by witches. These curses authorize demonic spirits to attack and torment a person in a special manner. Some people have curses of mental illnesses sent against them. Others, like Job, have curses of calamities and tribulations sent against them. In many superstitious and ignorant people, almost everything bad that happens in a person's life is blamed on a curse. However, the scriptures teach us differently.

Proverbs 26:2 says, *"As the bird by wandering, as the swallow by flying, so the curse causeless shall not come"* (King James Version). In other words, curses cannot just flit around in the air and by happenstance fall upon someone. A curse without a cause cannot alight. It will fail.

Nehemiah records a case of a curse failing. *"On that day they read from the Book of Moses in the hearing of the people, and in it was found written that no Ammonite or Moabite should ever come into the assembly of God, because they had not met the children of Israel with bread and water, but hired Balaam against them to curse them. However, our God turned the curse into a blessing"* (Nehemiah 13:1-2). Here we find that Ammonites and Moabites hired a man to send curses, or special assignments of devils, against the children of Israel as they traveled to the Promised Land. Because the Israelites were under the special protection of God, and were walking in the ways of God, the curse failed. In fact, the Lord turned the intended curse into a blessing.

Another curse failed when Goliath cursed David by his gods. Goliath lost his head over that curse. Years later when David was fleeing from his rebel son, Absalom, a descendant of Saul named Shimei came and threw stones at David, cursing him as his caravan traveled by. David patiently endured the cursing and would not let his men enter into retaliatory behavior. Because he left it in the hands of God, the curse failed.

The Bible mentions "generational curses" in Exodus 20:5, 34:7, Numbers 14:18 and Deuteronomy 5:9. It may sound unfair to some for God to punish children for the sins of their fathers. However, this is looking at it from an earthly perspective. God knows that the effects of sin are passed down from one generation to the next. When a father has a sinful lifestyle, his children are likely to have the same sinful lifestyle as well. That is why it is not unjust for God to punish sin to the third or fourth generation – because they were committing the same sins their ancestors were. However, it should be noted they were being punished for their own sins, not the sins of their ancestors.

Deuteronomy 24:16 specifically tells us that God does not hold children accountable for the sins of their parents. The fathers shall not be put to death for the children; neither shall the children be put to death for the fathers: every man shall be put to death for his own sin. The fact is Nimrod could have chosen to repent and serve God. Instantly, the curse against his family line would have been broken. He chose to build a tower for the worship of a demon named Marduke instead.

God told Moses to say to the people, *"Cursed shall you be when you come in, and cursed shall you be when you go out. The LORD will send on you cursing, confusion, and rebuke in all that you set your hand to do, until you are destroyed and until you perish quickly, because of the wickedness of your doings in which you have forsaken Me"* (Deuteronomy 28:19-20). By this passage we know there is a curse for disobedience. In other words, God has authorized special assignments against those who are disobedient.

Isn't it true when we came to Jesus Christ accepting Him as our personal Savior we were freed from every curse of sin? It is absolutely true in the same sense that Jesus died for all of mankind in order to save everyone. We know Jesus died for all mankind, but the fact remains that not everyone in the world is saved. Why is that true? It is true because although Jesus' death provided salvation for us, we still have to enter into the benefit of salvation through faith in Jesus Christ. You have to trust Jesus as your Savior and enter into your freedom from curses by a conscious action of your spirit and soul.

Isn't it also true that Jesus Christ took a gruesome beating upon his body so that by his brokenness your body can be made whole? I Peter 2:24 says in the latter part of the verse and quoting Isaiah 53:5, *"by whose stripes you were healed."* The past tense "were" is purposefully used by Peter, yet we know that in his day and certainly in our day, not everyone who is a Christian is sickness and disease free. How is that possible? By Jesus' stripes we were already healed, yet I know a brother who is very ill at this moment. Was Peter confused? No.

The truth is that Jesus has provided healing for us, but we have to enter into that provision by faith. James says, *"Is any sick among you? Let him call for the elders of the church and let them pray over him, anointing him with oil in the name of the Lord. And the prayer of faith shall save the sick, and the Lord shall raise him up"* (James 5:14-15a). Although Jesus' stripes won for us our healing, we must enter into our healing by faith, and apply that healing with action; a conscious decision of spirit and soul.

In the same way, Christ has redeemed us from the curse of the law, having become a curse for us (for it is written, *"Cursed is everyone who hangs on a tree"* (Galatians 3:13). Jesus won for us this freedom, but it has to be entered into by faith. Paul says, *"That the blessing of Abraham might come upon the Gentiles in Christ Jesus, that we might receive the promise of the Spirit through faith"* (Galatians 3:14). Even those born outside God's original promise to the descendants of Abraham can now receive this wonderful salvation, but it must be entered into by two methods. First, we must leave off trying to serve the law. The law was merely our tutor *"to bring us to Christ, that we might be justified by faith."* We have to enter this freedom from the curse by a conscious faith in Jesus Christ. Second, we must enter by faith into the free offering of grace by adopting a higher standard of behavior called love. It is one thing for a person to do something because he is being compelled to do it and it is quite another thing for that same person to do something because he loves to do it.

When I go home I kiss my wife, not because a law says I must do it, but because I love her and want to show her my love. Yes, we are freed from the curse of the law because of Jesus Christ, but we must enter into that freedom by consciously applying our faith in Jesus Christ. This is the higher way of love.

With all this freedom you would think anyone who comes to Jesus Christ would immediately be problem-free. In fact, that is not the case. Often that seems to be the point at which his problems escalate. When the devil owned the poor soul, he didn't worry about sending various torments because he had a firm grasp on the sinner by his constant sinful behaviors. However, when the same man came to Jesus Christ he had to begin to grapple with things that may have followed him from his past and from his parents' past.

In 1990 God began to deal with me about how to be free. I wanted to be free from guilt, free from condemnation and free from anger. Has anyone ever fought those things? We know from experience those things don't just pack up and leave when Jesus becomes our Savior. Experiencing the new birth was the first step, but it was not the final step.

I saw in me that something had to be done, so I started digging into the Word of God. God led me to that wonderful passage in John, "The truth shall make you free." In my quest to become free I had to deal with all the issues of my past. I wanted to be free from the guilt and condemnation that came on me as a result of my act of adultery. I knew I couldn't be completely free however, until I dealt with the root of what had gotten me there in the first place.

I began to remember those dreadful times in that little farmhouse and the results of my daddy's alcoholism. I was constantly tormented by the feeling that people were rejecting me because of my father. It caused anger to flare in me. After I left home and was married, my anger continued to flare. Often I asked the Lord to show me the root cause. In those weeks and months after the adultery became public, I vigorously searched and prayed to discover the roots in me because I wanted them out. I never wanted to come back to that place again. I certainly never wanted to see my family devastated like that again. I agonized before the Lord.

He brought me back to a night when I was just eight years old. My alcoholic daddy was under one of those special assignments—a curse from the enemy. He lived a life of rebellion and disobedience against God. My daddy was a small man who weighed less than 140 pounds, but he was physically strong and strong-willed. Working as a logging estimator, he was able to mentally calculate how many board feet of wood could be obtained out of an acre of forest. His potential however, was constantly thwarted by his desperate craving for alcohol. His daddy was an alcoholic, so my daddy just stayed under that same curse, under that same rebellion against God and he paid the same horrible price. My mother and we children paid the price too.

There was no electricity on our farm so our rough, board home was lit by kerosene lamps, and by flickering flames from the brick fireplace. Very early one morning while I was getting dressed, I listened to my father in the next room cursing my mother. With fear flooding my young mind I wanted to do something—anything—to stop the onslaught of my father's obscenities against my mother. I didn't move. I was too afraid. I felt my heart fill with shame.

As I grew, that fear and shame crystallized into anger and rage. From that time on, my first reaction to fear was anger. Every time I responded angrily I was reinforcing the power of the curse that had come upon me from my father and his father. Some years later the Lord gently uncovered this scene in my heart. I wept and repented of the shame and anger I had experienced. Even though I was a child and it was not my fault, I forgave myself for being unable to protect my mother.

I forgave my father for causing the whole mess. The rage in my heart died that day. I had entered into and applied to my life the freedom from the curse of anger Jesus had bought for me with his precious blood. From that day on, I was a more calm and patient person.

I once knew a man who had a terrible problem with lying. He prayed and accepted Jesus as his Savior, yet he continued to do what he had done for so many years. He had a lying spirit in him related to an adulterous affair he kept hidden for many years. This man could have come to the altar every service and prayed until he passed out, but he was not going to get delivered until he admitted, "I'm a liar." The first thing he had to do was admit he had a problem.

I had to admit that I had a problem with guilt, condemnation and anger. It was painful, but I had to admit it. Once I admitted that and came into the truth, I began to meditate on what the scriptures said about those things. I began to speak what the Word of God said, and confess what the Word of God said. I didn't speak what I was feeling. I began to speak what I was learning from the scriptures. I began to say that my guilt and condemnation had been washed away. I was made free by the truth of the Word of God. I learned that I could take the truth spoken to me by the scriptures, and activate it in my life by submission and meditation. I let it form me, and shape me. It began to manufacture or make me free.

Many Christians come to Jesus Christ for salvation, not for salvation from their sins, but salvation from eternal damnation of hell. They don't really want to give up their sins; they just want to add their religious experience with Jesus to their sins. The terrible mistake they are making is failure to appropriate in their lives what Jesus has done for them. They continue with the same bondages they used to have. They just trade company. Instead of running with sinners, they attend church and hide their sinful behavior at home. I see them on the street and they proclaim, "Oh Brother Gorman, I am so happy since Jesus came into my heart. My life is so changed." Their little son or daughter is standing there looking at them thinking, "What in the world is he talking about? He is just like he was last week!"

Too many people refuse to let Jesus into every area of their lives. By this they become hypocrites claiming to be saved, but saved from what? Their sins continue on in the same manner. These people need to firmly grasp the freedom Christ has won for them and then apply it to their lives.

When Jesus comes in, sin should go out. Sins of the flesh are usually the easiest to deal with after a person is truly born again. For many generations Gorman males were alcoholics. When I came to Jesus Christ, I rejected that sin and broke that curse by fully appropriating what Jesus had done for me. Psychiatrists will tell you that if your daddy is an alcoholic and your granddaddy is an alcoholic, if you start drinking you will almost without exception become an alcoholic. Yet here I was beating the odds and breaking this cycle. What happened?

The devils that had plagued my forefathers came to plague me too with the same old sin. I fell on my knees asking Jesus to help me. Those devils had to pack their bags and go because I was not going to participate in that sin. Their tricks and traps were not working for them.

What happened after that? I was left with other sinful behaviors, sins of the temperament that had to be confronted. My daddy had a fiery temper. That anger had a hold of my soul. It was written into my mind, will and emotions. If something happened to make me angry, I flared so big that it scared even me. I had to do something with that. I saw how the curse of rage had been passed into my generation, how devils came to tempt me to act out rage and anger. I could have stood there all day long saying, "There's no such thing as generational curses, so I'm just going to pretend I'm fine." Or, I could be honest with God by submitting myself to Him and appropriating His curse-breaking power in my life. That is how I was set free from a spirit of anger.

When we were first born again, we had to deal with the sins of the flesh. After a while, the Holy Spirit began to gently work with us to overcome the sins of the mind, will and emotions. We dealt with anger, wrath, malice, envy, gossip, lying, superstitions and those sorts of sins. As we continue to grow and mature in Christ, the Holy Spirit comes to teach us about sins of the spirit such as pride, hypocrisy and self-centeredness.

At each new level we can find threads that lead us back to generational sins. How many have ever said, "My grandmother was very superstitious so that's where I get it." Others have said, "My grandfather was very proud. That's where I get it." Some associate their sin with a certain people group. Drunkenness is often attributed to a person being

Irish. Stinginess is often attributed to a person being Scottish. The truth is these besetting sins that seem to follow certain family groups or people groups are caused by the curses, or special assignments sent against them while they are in disobedience. When a person is born again and becomes obedient to Jesus Christ, he must also enter into freedom from generational curses by faithfully applying the curse-breaking power of the blood of Jesus in his life.

You do not need a special church service to break off the curses in your life. You do not need a specially trained minister to help you break these curses. All you need to do is recognize that certain sins, ungodly behaviors, mindsets and beliefs are not bringing glory and honor to Jesus Christ. Repent of these and ask for the "wonder-working power in the precious blood of the Lamb" to work in your life to break the power of special demonic assignments against you. Then remain free by staying obedient to the Word of God and staying in constant fellowship with the Holy Spirit.

Jesus was teaching one day and *"as He said these things, many believed in Him (trusted, relied on, and adhered to Him.) So Jesus said to those Jews who had believed in Him, 'If you abide in my word (hold fast to my teachings and live in accordance with them), you are truly my disciples. And you will know the truth and the truth will set you free'"* (John 8:30-32, AMP).

When Jesus spoke to the Jewish disciples, they responded by arguing religious traditions with Him. *"They answered Him, 'We are Abraham's descendants, and have never been in bondage to anyone. How can You say, 'You will be made free'?"* (John 8:33). This religious spirit reigns in several cities I have ministered in. Hear what folks like this say today, "I go to church, but only on Easter and Christmas. I'm a real believer, but I don't think I have to go to church to prove it!" See, those folks are not being honest with themselves. They need to tell the truth to be free. The truth is they only go to church on Easter and Christmas to salve their guilty consciences and feel good for a little while.

They don't have a love relationship with the Lord. How do you think a wife would feel about her husband if he told other people, "Sure, I'm married! I visit her every Easter and Christmas." Does that sound like a marriage to you? Of course not! Yet, folks are content to show up at God's house once or twice a year and call themselves part of His family. It just doesn't wash!

Jesus heard this line of thinking out of the Jews who were not being honest with themselves. "We are Abraham's seed and not in bondage to any man!" Here they were in bondage so badly they were willing to kill people because of it. Paul was part of this crowd before he got converted to Jesus Christ. He had cast people in prison and given approval for people to be stoned to death.

Jesus didn't ignore their foolishness. He challenged them. Jesus answered them, *"Most assuredly, I say to you, whoever commits sin is a slave of sin"* (John 8:34). What Jesus was saying was, *"Do you really mean to tell me you're free; yet you're still sinning? Then if you are sinning you are bound by sin. How can you be free, and be bound at the same time?"* If you are going to be free you have to move into the truth and stop lying to yourself.

"And a slave does not abide in the house forever, but a son abides forever" (John 8:35). What was Jesus teaching them? He was saying, "Folks, the reason I know you are a servant to sin is because you have not moved into the truth to be made free. If you had moved into truth you would be free like a son. You're living like a servant to sin, not living like a son of God." Jesus challenged them because the only way you can be set free is to embrace the truth. Admit the truth. I am in bondage. I have dangerous and harmful curses in my life. I need the freedom that only Christ's truth can bring. Admit and then abide. Abide in the Word and let the Word abide in you. This will destroy anything that does not belong to Jesus. That is true freedom.

"Therefore, if the Son makes you free, you shall be free indeed" (John 8:36). Jesus was not finished with these people. He was teaching them that perhaps they had been freed from the burden of sin, but they were not free indeed. They were not free altogether. They needed to be made free from the bondages that came with that life of sin. The sin was gone, He was teaching them, but the bondages, the old ways of thinking, the religious traditions and their cultural biases were still apparent in their lives. Generational curses were still holding them to things that do not belong to a son of God. Some people are born again, but are tormented by the fear of death. They are free from the burden of sin, but not free from the bondage of fear. They need to be made free altogether. Free indeed!

My ancestors were Cherokee and Choctaw. They certainly did not live a life of freedom after the settlers began moving into their territories. They could say they were free all they wanted to, but a more powerful force was being brought to bear on their lives. They were held in bondage to many things by their own cultural and religious beliefs. These false beliefs kept them from understanding how to defend themselves against encroachment. They said they were free, but they were not free. They never admitted this until it was too late. Their numbers had been reduced by war and disease until they could not defeat the enemy. What really brought about their defeat? Was it the numbers of settlers or was it their own superstitions and cultural beliefs that held them even when they knew the enemy was growing stronger against them?

Some folks will stand with their cultural beliefs and religious traditions above their relationship with Jesus Christ. This is not freedom. This is the same kind of bondage Jesus was challenging in the Jews who were becoming His disciples. We have to stand with the truth of the Word of God no matter what attempts to bring us under a curse.

Christ has redeemed us from the curse of the law. Why did the Apostle Paul use the term Christ instead of the name Jesus? He wanted the people to understand it like this: "the Anointed One has redeemed you from the curse of the law." Christ is the Anointed One. What a powerful truth to know and proclaim! The Anointed One has redeemed you! *"It shall come to pass in that day that his burden will be taken away from your shoulder, and his yoke from your neck, and the yoke will be destroyed because of the anointing oil"* (Isaiah 10:27). Isaiah was pointing toward the day when Christ, the Anointed One, would obliterate the yoke of bondage.

If people realized what they were saying, they would not so readily use Christ's name in curses. Christ is not Jesus' last name. Christ is the title that was given to Him as the yoke breaker. It is the title that breaks the yoke. Paul is saying, *"Jesus Christ, the Anointed One, has come to minister to you and deliver you from the curse of the law. Being cursed because of disobedience to God can be broken if you enter into the truth of Jesus Christ."* You must enter into that truth. Jesus offering something to you and you consciously accepting it by applying it to your life, are two different things.

If someone pulled up in front of your house and left you a brand new car, what would you do? "Here is your new car," he may proclaim to you. "It is paid for, filled with gas and the title is in your name!" However, if you never accepted that car, but instead got into your shabby, old thing parked in your driveway, would that make any sense? You didn't really accept that the car was yours. Christians do this all the time. They leave the gifts God has given parked in the driveway of their lives never enjoying the freedom He offers.

Christ, the Anointed One, has redeemed you from the curse of the law. Curses can be broken in Jesus' name. You can be redeemed from what once held you in bondage, just like you can exchange that old wreck in your driveway for a brand new car, if you just accept the truth. Some Christians have not figured out that they have been made free. Faith comes by hearing and hearing by the Word of God. Hear it, accept it and then act on it.

If someone brought me a new car, I'd snap that door open, grab those keys, jump in that car and drive home with authority and confidence. If a policeman pulled me over, I'd reach into the glove compartment and pull out that title and say, "This is mine. That's my name right there. That's me!" I would have the authority to say it because I heard the truth, accepted the truth and then acted on the truth.

While I was a pastor my father requested my presence with him in the hospital. I listened as his doctor explained that my dad had a cancerous mass in his lungs. The doctor took me aside and said, "Son, your dad has only about three months to live." Then he laid his hand on my shoulder and told me, "I have never seen a father who admires his son as much as he admires you." No one will ever know how that statement moved me! My dad always had a difficult time paying me a compliment.

I went to the store, bought my daddy a Bible, and took it with me to the hospital. When I placed it on the little table, the pages fell open to the book of John. I began to read aloud, *"All that the Father gives Me will come to Me, and the one who comes to Me I will by no means cast out"* (John 6:37). My father looked up at me and asked, "Bud, does that mean me?" "Yes, Dad, it does mean you," I gladly told him. During the next few minutes I was able to lead my father to Jesus Christ. He lived several more months, so I was finally able to enjoy the Christian father for which I had so longed. Jesus gave us a love for each other that I wish every father and son could experience. The curse of alcohol and rage was broken because he entered into obedience to Jesus Christ.

Like my father and I did, you have to come to the place you recognize you've been redeemed. When you accept that, you will become free. Several years ago there was a man who sent me to a shop and wanted to buy me a suit, shirt and ties that matched. He wanted me to choose the color and get whatever I wanted. I told the manager at the shop the name of the man who had told me to go to that store and get fitted for some clothes and he would pay for them. He claimed he didn't know about the matter and said I couldn't do it. I asked him to call my benefactor, so he called him. Sure enough, I was telling the truth. I was to be the recipient of the new clothes. I could not declare ownership to my new wardrobe until I proved who would pay for them and proved who I was.

Jesus Christ has paid for our freedom from curses and all other bondages. We have to lay claim to what He has paid for. You have to know who you are in Christ Jesus. You have to know He has paid it all and has redeemed you.

"Cursed is everyone who hangs on a tree," wrote Paul in Galatians 3:13. Jesus was hung on a tree. He became a curse for us so that all the curses spoken against us passed down from generation to generation could be broken. Curses of sickness such as diabetes and heart disease can be broken by appropriating what Jesus has done for us. He has nailed them to the cross for us. You can stand and say, "Because of what Jesus did for me by becoming a curse for me, and by nailing the curses against me to the cross, I now stand free. I claim the freedom that comes from being an obedient child of God.

I can say those curses are broken over me. They may not pass on down to my children or my grandchildren in Jesus' name."

Jesus won the right for you to do this in the same way I won the right for my children and grandchildren to live free from demonic assignments of alcohol and rage. They have to maintain their freedom by living in obedience, but they are not plagued with special assignments of alcohol and rage like I was. They live in the freedom I appropriated to my own life.

We have to move into a spiritual state of understanding. There are curses that can be traced back to grandparents who dabbled in witchcraft, voodoo, all kinds of sin, false worship and all kinds of sexual sins. Those things may have followed you and plagued you for years. Jesus Christ broke those curses, but you will never benefit from it until you accept the fact that the curse was broken. The curse will not stop until an individual recognizes and accepts what Jesus has already done.

No one can break the curse until he or she enters into what Christ paid for. Those clothes were mine. When I finally got that truth across to the salesman, he let me have all that I came for. Why? He could not stand against truth. I could walk into the store and say, "I want this and I want that." I could do it because I was walking in the authority that my friend had given me by paying my bill. Your sins have been forgiven, so if you understand the curse has been broken, then you can act in authority.

American churches have been weakened because believers do not act with the authority that has been given to the church. People cry to God, "Give me authority, give me authority," and God says "You have authority. Satan has nothing over you because you have been liberated!"

Once the church embraces this truth, nothing will stop us. We will no longer be bound by besetting sins of the flesh, temperament or spirit because we will have entered into the freedom Jesus Christ won for us on the cross. Generational curses are real, but they do not have to be permanent. When a true believer stands against those things that have repeated themselves down through the generations, those special assignments can be cancelled in the name of Jesus Christ.

CHAPTER ELEVEN:
FIGHT THROUGH OPPRESSION

Harsh Egyptian taskmasters were oppressing the children of Israel millenniums ago. *"And the LORD said: 'I have surely seen the oppression of My people who are in Egypt, and have heard their cry because of their taskmasters, for I know their sorrows'"* (Exodus 3:7). Aren't you glad the Lord knows your sorrows? He also knows when the enemy comes to oppress His people. One of the toughest battles Christians fight is oppression. Oppression is a mean thing.

Oppression, in other words using power to disempower, silence and subordinate the children of Israel, was generations in the making. Why not? The Egyptian pharaohs were privileged and further empowered by their evil oppression. For generations they disempowered and subordinated descendants of Jacob in harsh and bitter servitude while God remained silent. God was silent, but not blind.

The children of Israel were not the first, nor would they be the last people group to experience oppression. Black slaves in America were oppressed with the institution of slavery. Irish peasants were oppressed with the system of landlords. In other words, whoever had the land could lord it over whoever did not have the land. Most races and religions have faced oppression at one time or another down through history. The children of Israel faced the cruel oppression of their host nation for four hundred years. One day God

193

shattered His silence with the crackling fire of a burning bush. Deliverance was at hand.

"So I have come down to deliver them out of the hand of the Egyptians, and to bring them up from that land to a good and large land, to a land flowing with milk and honey, to the place of the Canaanites and the Hittites and the Amorites and the Perizzites and the Hivites and the Jebusites. Now therefore, behold, the cry of the children of Israel has come to me, and I have also seen the oppression with which the Egyptians oppress them. Come now, therefore, and I will send you to Pharaoh that you may bring my people, the children of Israel, out of Egypt" (Exodus 3:8-10). The Lord God hears and sees, and you better believe He is going to act. Psalm 34:15-16 says, *"The eyes of the Lord are on the righteous, and His ears are open to their cry. The face of the Lord is against those who do evil, to cut off the remembrance of them from the earth."*

The cries of the righteous men and women like Amram and Jochebed, Moses' courageous parents, and probably many others, had ascended to heaven. God heard their cries. Eventually, Egypt's cup of wrath was full. God turned His face toward His children. Suddenly the balance of power changed.

Thousands of years later, the balance of power shifted again because of who Jesus Christ was. Luke recorded in Acts 10:38, *"how God anointed Jesus of Nazareth with the Holy Spirit and with power, who went about doing good and healing all who were oppressed by the devil, for God was with Him."* Satan's empire began to crumble when saints like Simeon and Anna cried to the Lord. The Lord heard their cries and responded by sending His only Son *"that whosoever believes on Him shall not perish, but have everlasting life"* (John 3:16). The oppression of the enemy, the move by Satan to disempower, marginalize and silence the human creation of God was broken. Jesus came and people were healed – body, soul and spirit.

The people who really want something from God are the people who press in to receive from God. Through Moses, God was ready to deliver a people from the cruel hand of the oppressor, but if there had been Israelites who didn't want to come out, they could have stayed. God heard their cries and responded by setting the wheels in motion to deliver them. However, the descendants of Jacob still had a responsibility to respond to their deliverance by moving out in faith.

What if some had holed up in their little shanties and said, "I don't think God is really doing anything? I think I'll just stay and work in the mud again tomorrow." What foolishness! God was providing a way for them, but they had the responsibility to respond in faith. God was setting them free from their oppressors, but they still faced the giants in the new land. They were not going to have freedom handed to them on a silver platter. They were going to have to exercise their faith, put their feet on the ground and take a sword into their hands. Oppression doesn't go away just because you want it to.

God wants to bring you to a land flowing with milk and honey…and giants. You can keep two if you defeat one. Some folks let the giants walk all over them, letting go of the milk and honey. God wants to deliver you, but you must remember between you and every promise is a demon you will need to defeat. Demons of oppression specialize in keeping Christians from their Promised Land.

God knew the children of Israel could not fight the Canaanites in the wilderness if they were afraid. He knew He would have to first deliver them from the oppressive spirits of fear. He took them the long way around through the wilderness in order to reveal Himself to them as a good Father, a trustworthy Father, and as a strong and competent defender. He needed them to get rid of the fear and begin to move with Him in faith. They were faced with trial after trial which became opportunity after opportunity for them to defeat the spirit of fear. Fear and faith cannot peacefully coexist in the same heart. The oppressive spirits of fear were defeated as they moved in faith with their Father.

For you did not receive the spirit of bondage again to fear, but you received the Spirit of adoption by whom we cry out, *"Abba, Father"* (Romans 8:15). When I was in school I used to get into fights nearly every day. There were some boys I fought who just wouldn't stay whipped! I had to fight them again the next day. Some Christians are living like that. They seem to have to fight the same enemies over and over again. The Apostle Paul was trying to teach the early Christians that the spirit of bondage, like that which was on the children of Israel, did not have to remain on them if they would enforce something different. Things that you have allowed to enslave you might not stay gone just because you went to the altar. Something more has to happen.

Do you want to get rid of fear? If you don't accept adoption, you're going to go right back into fear. What does adoption mean? Adoption means that you are brought into the family of God, all your debts are paid and any evil you have ever done is paid for. Paul stated it beautifully, *"having wiped out the handwriting of requirements that was against us, which was contrary to us. And He has taken it out of the way, having nailed it to the cross"* (Colossians 2:14). Gone forever! If you move into adoption, you don't have to worry anymore about whether or not you will be cared for.

You must embrace adoption in the same way the street child who gets adopted must embrace his new family. He must be willing to be cared for by them. He no longer has to dig in the garbage can for his meals. He no longer has to find a box to sleep in at night. He has a new family with a new father and mother who are willing to provide for him. Remember when Jesus said the lily is not worried and the sparrow is not worried about these things? Your Heavenly Father knows you have need of these things. Fear evaporates when Christian people begin to understand that God has accepted responsibility for them.

When I married my wife, she had a little boy whose father had drowned. I assumed responsibility for that child. My son never had to worry where his food was coming from, or where his clothes were coming from. He never had to worry about where he was going to sleep or if he would have a place to sleep because I became his father. I assumed those responsibilities and I took care of him. When you became a Christian your Heavenly Father accepted you as an heir and joint heir with Jesus Christ. He adopted you into His family, so you no longer have to fret and worry. Your Heavenly Father is watching over you taking care of your every need.

Now all you have to do is say, "Abba Father, my Father, my Daddy I need this." My little boy has grown to be an adult with children and grandchildren of his own, but he still knows when he calls Dad and asks for something, if I have it he'll get it and if I don't have it, I will try to secure it for him and see that he gets it. My boy embraced adoption and because of that, he doesn't fear. The spirit of bondage has no hold on him because I treat him the same as my two biological children and he has embraced adoption. Many people are oppressed by the enemy today because they don't really know where they stand with their Heavenly Father. They don't understand adoption.

We have to move out of the mentality of letting the devil beat us down and make us think we are still in Egypt. You were brought out of Egypt and you've been adopted by a Father, who is well able to care for you. All your debts are paid. Nobody can lay claim to you because you are free. The Spirit bears witness that we are the children of God. When you accept this truth you have a deeply settled peace in your heart. I don't get up in the morning and worry about whether I'm saved or not. If I sin, I am not worrying about whether God will forgive me or not. I'm His child, not a bastard. I'm a child and because of that He will chastise me if He has to, but I am still His child. That gives me blessed assurance, peace and confidence. I know the oppressor has no power over me.

Many times we get into bondage in our Christian walk. Young people especially have this problem. They are filled with fear and have a slavery mentality. Why do we do that? Let me explain. Bill knew he needed to get rid of his drugs, but he decided he was going to achieve deliverance by his own efforts. That is one way people get into bondage. That's why more people can't get delivered from smoking. Instead of throwing themselves on the mercy of God and letting God deliver them, they decide they're going do it themselves. That little cigarette has defeated more people than you can count. An individual may think, "I'm going to be what I need to be. I'll defeat this on my own." He tries real hard, but becomes oppressed by guilt when he cannot do it on his own. Satan takes advantage of this. He begins to accuse him and enslave him with fear.

Some people are able to conquer besetting sins of the flesh by the sheer force of their own will. This gives them a false impression of their spiritual power. It is one thing to be set free and then another to be able to flow in the Spirit. Paul asked, "Would you explain who came in and bewitched you? You started in the spirit, but now are you going to try to finish in the flesh? Are you going to try to become what you ought to be by your own efforts?" The truth is you cannot do it. It is by the Spirit that you learn to walk in the Spirit, pray in the Spirit and live in the Spirit.

The Holy Spirit is the only one who can help you. You can't deliver yourself. You can't correct your sinful nature. That is why the scripture says, *"Can the Ethiopian change his skin or the leopard its spots? Then may you also do good who are accustomed to do evil"* (Jeremiah 13:23). You can't change what you are inside, but God can. God takes the Word and the

Spirit and begins to work on you. He works on you by changing you from the inside. That begins to reflect on the outside. People are oppressed going and coming and are under guilt and self-condemnation because they are not overcoming something they need to overcome. They try to do it on their own and fall under the oppression of the enemy.

Other people come under oppression because they are constantly trying to please someone else. I love my wife, but my goal in life is not to please her. As wonderful as she is, she still has different moods for different days. She also has changeable desires. If I had as my primary goal to please her, I wouldn't know from one day to the next what to do. However, I know if I please the Lord that will please my wife more than anything because she also loves the Lord and also desires to please Him. We're at peace with each other in our ultimate goal, which is to please the Lord Jesus Christ. Pleasing the Lord brings peace, while trying to please other humans too often brings oppression.

Another way Christians come under oppression is by feelings of uselessness. We are all created with certain gifts, talents, inclinations and strengths which exist to bring glory and honor to Jesus. If we begin to feel useless and valueless, the enemy begins to fuel those thoughts until despair takes over. Elderly Christians are particularly susceptible to this trick of the enemy. They retire and begin to putter around the house doing all the chores they always thought about doing. First thing you know the chores are done and the man or woman has less and less to do every day.

When God placed Adam and Eve in the Garden of Eden, He commanded them to tend the garden. They had a job and a purpose. Work is therapeutic. Perhaps the elderly cannot physically work like they used to, but there is always something that can be done. Elderly Christians can volunteer at their church food pantry, tutor young children or volunteer to rock babies in the hospital nurseries. They can work at the local library, or plant a garden and give the produce away to the hungry. There are as many things to do as there are people to do them. Satan begins to oppress the elderly by making them feel useless. They withdraw from society and because they feel like they are on the outside looking in, they continue to fall under the power of oppression.

A good rule of thumb is to constantly consider we all have to give an account of the deeds done in our bodies whether they are good or evil. When I come to the end of my journey, I desire to be able to say to my Lord, "I have endeavored to be obedient to your command, to occupy until you come." I've been actively ministering for more than 60 years, and I intend to be ministering when Jesus sends the angels to take me home. I refuse to fall under the oppression of the feelings of uselessness.

The enemy uses oppression to prey on your weaknesses. Until your inner man becomes strong, the outer flesh will rule you. The inner man becomes strong through prayer, meditation, the study of the Word; and living and walking in the Spirit. As you live and walk in the Spirit you will be strengthened in your inner man. Then you will be able to overcome the flesh. God knew that the slaves pouring out of

Egypt really and truly didn't know how to fight. If He had taken them straight from Egypt, the Canaanites would have destroyed the whole bunch of them. God took them into the wilderness, not to teach them to fight, but to teach them to trust. He led them. When the cloud moved, they moved. They learned to trust Him for manna, water and meat. Whenever a plague came, they had to trust Him to stop the plague.

When fiery serpents came among them, He taught them to trust Him for deliverance and healing. He had them make a brass pole with the image of a serpent lifted up high and those who looked on it were healed. It is still true today. When you look to Jesus Christ you will receive help, but if you do not look to Jesus you will get into trouble. Your solution is to keep your eyes on Jesus. If we start out in our own strength and fail, condemnation comes. The next thing you know the enemy trots in with a horde of demons, nets of guilt and self-recriminations and tries to haul us off to Egypt again.

You cannot conquer sin by human effort. You can only conquer sin by the blood of Jesus Christ. You cannot come out of the wilderness by your own efforts. Only one can get you out of the wilderness and that is the Holy Spirit. The Israelites would have never survived if not for the pillar of fire by night and cloud by day that guided them to the Promised Land.

The Christian life is lived from the neck up. If Satan can oppress your thoughts, then he can oppress you. If he can do that, then he can depress you. Eventually he can even possess you. Your thought life is either a playground for the devil, or a place that glorifies God. If your thoughts were played on a big screen in Times Square would you be ashamed? Oppression brings in fear, doubt and anxiety. Suddenly, you are overwhelmed and incapable of fighting off the attacks of the enemy.

Some Christians become suicidal after falling into oppression and depression. That shouldn't be happening. The enemy comes and possesses their minds until murdering themselves seems like a good idea. Some people today are oppressed and then depressed. Next, a spirit of hopelessness sets in until they are so possessed Satan is calling the shots. They suddenly think taking a gun and shooting up a school or church makes complete sense. The devil has possessed their minds by telling them they would be better off if they were out of this world. Oppression led to depression. Depression led to possession. That is why it is so important to be healed from oppression by letting the Word of God be the author of your thought life.

Jesus went about doing good and healing all that were oppressed by the devil. Because He is the truth, He brought the truth into lives and the oppression from the devil was defeated. Every time the devil tries to say nobody cares and throws this thought out, "Nobody understands you," I want you to know there is a Savior who understands you. He knows every hair on your head, every pain, every thought and every imagination. He knows you! You might say, "You don't know my family situation." I would say to you, "Change families!" The adoption papers are already drawn up and the Father will adopt you into His family. The devil makes people believe they have no one, in order to drive them into despair so they will destroy themselves. But God anointed Jesus with the Holy Spirit and with power for the express purpose of healing all who were oppressed of the devil.

People who struggle with sin are not the only ones who can come under oppression. Anytime a pastor tries to accomplish his ministry responsibilities without the leadership of the Holy Spirit, he may build an audience, but he will never build a church. He may become discouraged and defeated and fall into oppression. Tragically, he may make the mistake of remaining in the pulpit. During my years of ministry, I have rebuked some pastors for their attitude toward their congregation.

Some city folks won't understand this analogy, but a real good farmer can taste cow's milk and tell you what she's been eating. If she has been into mushrooms, you can taste it. If she has been into bitter weeds, you'll taste it. When I preach, the very things I have meditated on will be evidenced. If I don't have love, but am full of anger, bitterness and resentment, then I am exposing the congregation to that. It is like walking into a room to visit someone who has the flu and high fever and expecting not to get sick. When preachers get oppressed, they need to stay out of the pulpit until they're healed. If they don't, it will affect the entire congregation.

Oppression has no mercy. Oppression is out there seeking somebody who is open to it. Satan goes about like a roaring lion. It may be fear that's following you, looking for an opportunity to pounce on you and bring you under its control. I thank God for my wife who helped me while I was going through the darkest hour of my life because, when I became oppressed, I just wanted to withdraw. Oppression relentlessly hounded me, but my wife stood in the gap for me. I was mercifully delivered.

Many Christians opt out of church on Sunday saying they just don't feel well. Often the truth is, there is nothing physically wrong with them; they have just come under an oppression of the enemy. Oppression moves in and becomes heaviness that makes you not want to do anything like comb your hair, take a bath or clean the house. Oppression attempts to take away everything that would make you feel better. My wife could be having a bad day. If somebody picks her up and takes her to have her hair and nails done, before you know it, she perks up and is joyful again.

The devil jumps on some and makes them say, "I don't care. I don't care what I look like." That is the start of a downward spiral, but the truth is the devil still cannot control you by oppression. He can only make you begin to think thoughts he wants you to think. Those uncontrolled thoughts will open the door to oppression.

Once into oppression, the devil will try to open you up for possession. Many a person has embraced a critical attitude until they became oppressed. They began to think nothing and no one is good enough. They critiqued and evaluated everything. Ever notice how those with a critical attitude will tend to congregate together? They try to justify themselves by getting others to agree with their attitudes. If you bring fifteen oppressed people into a congregation and invite the congregation to go around and greet each other, in an amazingly short period of time all of those critical people will congregate together.

Christians under the oppression of gossip will gravitate to one another and feed on gossip from one another. Satan knows this. He has observed human nature for thousands of years. Although we have authority over him, you can't walk around with your head in the air thinking that he doesn't have a plan. He has a plan and that plan is to oppress you, to make you a slave in order to silence and disempower you. God had quite a task when He brought the children of Israel out of Egypt. He was trying to get a bunch of slaves to believe there was a God who was for them, who would fight for them and who would do the impossible for them. He had to allow them to experience different challenges in order to teach them that He was faithful and capable of leading them from bondage to victory.

When someone is down for so long, nobody can pick them up in one day. When the Israelites could see the consistency of God's care, they began to arise. This is what must happen to the body of Christ. There are too many Christians who are oppressed. We need to recognize and discern that spirit. If you sense someone is being oppressed of the devil, walk up to them and start saying things like, "I appreciate you. I like that shirt. You really look nice in that color." When you start moving into their lives with words of acceptance and appreciation, you are breaking that spirit of oppression against them. They may just look at you blankly, but you should keep intruding lovingly into their thought processes with words of appreciation. By this simple strategy you can begin to lift them up out of the mire of oppression until they can begin to think new thoughts.

Everyone has a problem they wish they didn't have, but how they deal with that problem determines whether they will be oppressed or depressed or whether they will march on to victory. Do I feel I'm perfect? No! Does Satan try to point out my faults? Absolutely! How do I respond? I say, "Satan, God knew everything about me when He chose me. There is nothing I do or say that surprises God. He chose me, He saved me, He filled me with His Spirit and called me into the ministry." If Satan keeps pressing me, I remind him, "Jesus loves me. Jesus cares about me. Jesus wants me. Jesus is not ashamed of me and not ashamed to be identified with me."

Oppression is a real enemy and if I were to listen to the devil he would take me right into depression. I choose not to go there. Every person who is depressed was first oppressed. A cloud came over them, a gray heaviness, and then the devil kept badgering them until they believed a lie, any lie. It might have been an accusation that they aren't saved, or they've done something wrong or they're to blame for someone being mad at them. If they stay under this lie, the oppression sets in with power and the next stop on the freight train of destruction is depression.

No one wants to willfully and purposefully fall into depression. In fact, more often it is a gentle slide downhill from oppression to depression. Once the believer slides into depression, it is difficult to climb out. Our mind constantly adjusts to what it believes is true. Violent crime victims survive often because they tell themselves that it is not so bad.

Domestic violence survivors often stay with their abusers a long time because they constantly adjust their expectations until they accept hell on earth without complaint. The mind adjusts itself to oppression by saying, "This is just the way it is."

The truth of the matter is that our standard of living must not be what others do to us or say about us, but what Jesus has done for us and what He says about us. If that standard is always lifted up in our hearts and minds we can measure what is happening and reject what doesn't come up to the standard. Once we realize what we are thinking and feeling is actually a result of oppression against our mind or spirit, we can position ourselves to fight against the oppressor. Often the thought of fighting seems impossible. We feel we just do not have the energy. We can't seem to get up.

That is when the deadliest force against the enemy should be used because it not only puts the devil to flight, but it also builds our spirits and our faith. This deadly force which Christians can learn to use in the battle against oppression is sincere praise. Praising God is not always easy.

Anyone can praise God when everything is going right. But when things are rough, then it takes real effort and determination to praise God. In the midst of trials, it is hard not to indulge in self-pity. It is hard to avoid feeling sorry for yourself. However, praise, even if it is a sacrifice of praise, is your most effective response to a situation that could bring on fear, doubt, discouragement and depression. God honors a sacrifice because a sacrifice honors God. Hebrews 13:15 says,

"Therefore by Him let us continually offer the sacrifice of praise to God, that is, the fruit of our lips, giving thanks to His name."

Notice that the Bible calls praise a sacrifice. Anytime you exert special effort at the expense of your own comfort or enjoyment for the sake of pleasing or obeying God, He will honor that sacrifice. Whether your effort involves prayer, the study of the Word, attending the house of God, service and ministry to others, financial giving or offering praise, God delights in a sacrifice which comes from a sincere heart. A sacrifice says to God and to the world, "God is important enough to me that I want to do something for Him that costs me something." Difficult situations can beat your faith down until it is almost impossible to believe that God will answer your prayers unless you take definite, positive action. More than anything else, the sacrifice of praise can build up your faith to receive victory from God.

Praise may begin with thanking God, not necessarily for anything He has done for you, but thanking Him for who He is. Praise must always be based on God's immutable attributes. This easily reminds us of what He has done for us. Praise often recalls what God has done. When you are sick, troubled or facing battles, take a moment and recall what God has done for you. Then praise Him for those things. The sacrifice of praise may mean beginning to praise the Lord even with tears coursing down your cheeks, with pain deep in your heart and with anguish of soul and spirit. Although you don't feel like it, you lift up your voice to God and say, "I praise you because you have shown your love for me. I praise you because you have saved me. I praise you for the things you have done."

Think about making a notebook of God's blessings. Write down the date He saved you and the date He filled you with His Spirit. Over time, you will have pages and pages of blessings you can refer back to in times of trouble. Just begin to praise your way through the lists.

Praise lifts you above circumstances. Meditating on your problems, indulging in self-pity, self-recriminations or mental assaults against others will not solve your problems. You must rise above the circumstances which are defeating you. The only way to accomplish this is to reach up and catch hold of the hand of Him who is higher than you. As you begin to praise God and rejoice in Him, He will lift you up above your sorrows and into an environment of victory.

One man who learned the value of praising God was King David. When the storms of life were coming in, threatening to destroy him, David cried to God, *"From the end of the earth I will cry to You, when my heart is overwhelmed; lead me to the rock that is higher than I"* (Psalm 61:2). Praise centers our attention on the Lord rather than on our problems.

Zoologists tell us that some species of snakes can literally charm birds down out of trees into their striking range. If one of these snakes can get a bird to look at it, the power of its hypnotic, unblinking gaze can cause the bird to freeze or even move closer. Then, in an instant, the snake strikes and the bird is killed and eaten. That's what happens to many people. They get their eyes on their enemy and on their problems until the thing becomes an obsession to them. It becomes a magnet which draws them to their own destruction. But through praise we can rise above problems and circumstances to see things as they really are—the way God sees them. From the praise perspective, problems do not look nearly as big, and suddenly our faith rises to believe that God will meet us and help us.

Praise helps us live in the moment. One of Satan's most effective weapons is causing us to wonder about what will happen tomorrow. What if this happens? What if that doesn't happen? Trying to walk across tomorrow's bridge while you are still on today's street will stretch you too far. You will fall to your destruction. Praise can help you live victoriously today. Praise helps you rest today in the arms of the One who holds tomorrow. If you will live this moment in the fullness of the presence of God, He will give you the courage and faith to face tomorrow. Through praise you can defy the doubts of the enemy and be victorious.

Sometimes people fail to receive victories from God because they dwell on their own merit instead of on the mercies of God. On the one hand, some people try to tell God, "I've done this and that, and given this and that and sacrificed this and that," implying that God must hear their prayers because of it. God hears your prayers based on your faith and the blood of His Dear Son, Jesus Christ. Victory comes through the grace, righteousness and goodness of God, not through any merits of mankind.

On the other hand, others feel that they cannot receive anything from God because they are so unworthy. They let the devil beat them and accuse them with their failures or shortcomings. To receive from God, get your mind off what you deserve or don't deserve and get your mind on who God really is. Start praising Him because He is merciful and gracious, longsuffering and abounding in goodness and truth. You can praise Him based on His own description of Himself, which He declares in Exodus 34:6, *"And the LORD passed before him and proclaimed, 'The LORD, the LORD God, merciful and gracious, longsuffering, and abounding in goodness and truth.'"*

In my opinion, one of the greatest songs of praise is, *"How Great Thou Art."* I once heard someone ask, "Doesn't God already know how great He is?" Of course He does! But He wants to know that you do, and He wants you to tell Him. Why? For three reasons: it brings Him honor for you to praise Him, it builds your own faith in Him as you confess how great He is and it moves your eyes from your problem to your solution. Praise is the lethal force Christians must apply against oppression. When the enemy comes in like a flood, lift up a standard of praise to honor Jesus Christ. The enemy will quickly be defeated.

Christians who are living their lives mentally, emotionally and spiritually oppressed are missing out on some of the greatest benefits of salvation. Salvation was not just for your eternity. Salvation is for your here and now! You can be saved from oppression by understanding the victory Jesus Christ has won, and by positioning yourself mentally, emotionally and spiritually in that victory. He is Name Above all Names. He is Mighty God, Prince of Peace. He is our Redeemer. He is our Victor. He has won for us the position of overcomer just in the same way He won for us the position of being born again. We have to choose by faith to enter into that victory in the same way we had to choose by faith to enter into salvation. Then when the oppression comes through devilish attacks, we fight off the oppression from the position of Christ as Victor.

God had to lead the children of Israel into the wilderness to teach them who God really was, and to convince them that God really wanted to love them and care for them as His dear children. Those like Joshua and Caleb learned this lesson and were swept into the Promised Land, receiving their inheritance and enjoying the fruits of victory. They believed and acted on their beliefs by fighting for their victory and praising God for everything He had done. They broke the power of the oppressor by embracing their adoption. They believed their Father and fought because He said they could win. A fierce battle Christians will fight is against oppression, but with courage and faith in their Heavenly Father, it is a fight they can win.

CHAPTER TWELVE:
DESCENT INTO DEPRESSION

When oppression has fully developed in the thought life and becomes depression, an abnormal thing may occur. Instead of the thought life being tormented, the sufferer may simply not think at all. He begins to experience long periods of "blankness" or "numbness of the mind." If you ask him what he is feeling, he cannot tell you. He feels blank. His mind is a blank. This is a dangerous trap of the devil. A blank slate is a perfect place upon which the devil can begin to write all sorts of dangerous and ungodly thoughts.

Israel's King Saul is a perfect example of one who made the descent from oppression to depression and ultimately possession. Scriptures tell us that the prophet Samuel was old. He had turned some of the administrative duties of the nation over to his sons, Joel and Abiah. Unfortunately, they accepted bribes and did not walk in a godly manner. The elders of Israel gathered and demanded a king. Samuel was displeased, but the Lord determined He would give them what they requested. And the LORD said to Samuel, *"Heed the voice of the people in all that they say to you; for they have not rejected you, but they have rejected Me, that I should not reign over them"* (I Samuel 8:7).

The Lord sent to Israel what they really wanted. Saul, son of Kish was head and shoulders taller than other men. He was muscular and good looking. He was powerful. He was chosen king. What a thrill it must have been for this young man! One day he was wandering the hillsides looking for his father's donkeys, and the next day he was being told by the famous prophet, Samuel, that he had been chosen king. He was called to be a worker for God. In short order he received revelation, and even experienced the power of the Holy Spirit. Then the Spirit of the LORD will come upon you, and you will prophesy with them and be turned into another man (I Samuel 10:6). The people wanted a king and, although God knew the end from the beginning, He let them have their king.

The coronation was splendid. The people rejoiced and were in awe. Now they would be like other nations. They would be ruled by a king rather than this obscure God who could not be seen. Surely King Saul felt a rush of pride and pleasure in what had suddenly transpired in his life. After the coronation, he returned to his home in Gibeah, along with a band of faithful followers. *"But some rebels said, 'How can this man save us?' So they despised him, and brought him no presents. But he held his peace"* (I Samuel 10:27). Although King Saul held his peace, I believe it is possible this rejection is where the seeds of his destruction were sown.

Rejection can be painful and oppressive. I remember as a young boy growing up in Arkansas how often I felt the harshness of rejection. My father's drunkenness carried a stigma that followed me everywhere. The sting of rejection made me seethe with anger.

Perhaps King Saul began to seethe as well. Nahash, the Ammonite, came up and encamped against Jabesh-gilead. His wicked oppression of the people caused men to run weeping to King Saul. He was quick to action. Saul cut his own oxen to pieces, and sent the bloody parts by messengers throughout all of Israel saying that if the men did not respond to fight with him, he would cut up their oxen too. In short order, he had gathered an army of Israelites.

The next morning, he and his army had slaughtered the Ammonites and saved Jabesh-gilead. What a triumph! In fact, the people were so excited they wanted to renew the kingdom and celebrate King Saul all over again. As with any group of people, some grumblers murmured around the edges of town. Offended, some men suggested putting to death Saul's nay-sayers, but Saul rejected that idea and focused on celebrating his vindication. He was the darling of Israel, the subject of ballads and the toast of feasts.

During his second year, King Saul's son, Jonathan, led an attack on a garrison of Philistines which was surprisingly successful. However, they had stirred up an awful hornet's nest. The Philistines came down on them with a vengeance. The people hid themselves in caves, and thickets, rocks and high places and in pits.

Desperate to regain his stature and bring order out of chaos, King Saul offered the burnt offering instead of waiting for the prophet Samuel. As soon as he breached this spiritual protocol, Samuel appeared and delivered to King Saul harsh correction. *"And Samuel said to Saul, 'You have done foolishly. You have not kept the commandment of the LORD your God, which He commanded you. For now, the LORD would have established your kingdom over Israel forever. But now your kingdom shall not continue. The LORD has sought for Himself a man after His own heart, and the LORD has commanded him to be commander over*

His people, because you have not kept what the LORD commanded you'" (I Samuel 13:13-14). The Lord turned His back on Saul as did Samuel. In two short years, everything he had gained turned to dust in his disobedient hands. Samuel later said that God would have preferred obedience rather than sacrifice.

Imagine the onslaught of oppressive spirits that attacked King Saul after his rejection. Surely he began to think thoughts that were not worthy of the ways of God. Perhaps the anger that seethed toward his critics now turned toward Samuel and God. Resentment and bitterness is fueled by anger and rejection. Saul sickened his own spirit with this poison. His descent into depression had begun.

Did you know depression can come hand in hand with anger? A cavity filled with anger manifests itself in different ways, but most often it manifests itself as depression. Psychologists sometimes refer to depression as "anger turned inward." Instead of focusing anger where it belongs, the sufferer simmers with anger, but never acknowledges it and certainly never asks for deliverance from it.

People are surprised to find out Jesus once acted in anger. He became so angry because of the wickedness happening in the temple that He plaited a whip and drove out the moneychangers. He shouted, *"It is written, My house shall be called a house of prayer; but you have made it a den of thieves!"* Jesus was angry, but He focused His anger where it belonged and corrected the problem.

Too many men are angry at their bosses, so they come home and mistreat their wife and kids. Many women are angry at their husband for spending too much time with the guys, so they spend too much money shopping. Incorrectly focusing our anger or acting in an aggressive manner is not the way to deal with anger. Jesus dealt with it by correcting what was wrong. He set everyone straight, and then got back to His Father's business. In the very next verse after His zealous action the scripture said, *"Then the blind and the lame came to Him in the temple, and He healed them"* (Matthew 21:14). He purged the temple of the business of man so He could get down to the business of God.

Some people simply choose not to express their anger at all. They shut up and shut down. Suicide can occur because a person suppresses anger until thoughts of helplessness overwhelm him. Next, thoughts of worthlessness rush in to make a person believe that it doesn't matter if they live or die. But it does matter. And it surely matters to God. Oppression opens us to depression, which if not dealt with, will gradually slide a person into possession.

The spiral into suicide is: oppression, depression, (including thoughts of helplessness or worthlessness) then possession. I believe suicides often result from deep depression, which opens the door for demonic possession. Demonic spirits cause a person to believe that there is no way out and that death is a good choice.

When one cannot control or change present or past circumstances it may open a door of anger which produces depression. King Saul faced this door, but instead of falling on the mercy of God and crying out for help, he continued to entertain ungodly thoughts until one day possession took place. But the Spirit of the LORD departed from Saul, and a distressing spirit from the LORD troubled him" (I Samuel 16:14). Why did God permit an evil spirit to trouble him? King Saul justified his actions, disobeyed, refused to repent, seethed with anger, embraced oppression and fell into depression. This was an open door for an evil spirit. After the death of Samuel, Saul contacted a witch and asked her to bring up Samuel by her witchcraft so he could inquire of him. Somehow this warped and perverted action seemed right in Saul's eyes. That's how far his depression had taken him.

What could have halted his downward spiral? The repentance and forgiveness techniques that I shared in an earlier chapter could have changed the course of Saul's life and restored him to his right mind. A noted psychologist reported that approximately 95% of people who come to his clinic for therapy are depressed due to repressed anger toward an abuser or toward oneself. In fact, he encourages clients to learn forgiveness as a way to deal with the anger we feel from the effects of what he calls, "jerk abuse." In his experience, "anger and depression are close relatives" (Meier, Paul, M.D. *"Don't Let Jerks Get the Best of You,"* Thomas Nelson, 1993).

We all have occasion to deal with difficult people who love to "pull our strings" or who find that last, raw nerve and are intent on jumping up and down on it. That's why I constantly remind people that "a day without repentance is like eating from the same dirty plate all day long." We need to constantly repent of our anger and forgive difficult people.

Christians often seek out counselors or ministers for deliverance when what they really need to do is spend time alone with God in sincere repentance and forgiveness. If the poison of repressed anger and the pain of rejection were removed, more than likely the depression would lift.

I am reminded of when I grew up on the farm in Arkansas. My family raised pigs. We had a nanny whose name was Aunt Polly Moore. She was in her eighties, thin, with short, gray hair. She was sixteen years old when she was freed from slavery. Aunt Polly had little formal education, but worlds of wisdom. She always helped us children with the hogs. She taught us how to pour lye in their food to kill the parasites. "Oh, they'll squeal," she would say, "but it'll be good for them." In the next pen there was a hog trough without lye in the meal. One great big sow knew that was where the better tasting food was; so she tore down the fence and headed to that trough. Every time Aunt Polly treated the hog food with lye, that old sow would break down the fence and head for the other trough. One day as I was trying to repair the fence, Aunt Polly hollered to me, "Baby, you don't need a stronger fence. Just move the hog feed!"

I often remember that lesson when I deal with people who are oppressed and depressed. If a person will remove the anger or bitterness by true repentance and forgiveness, they will inevitably discover that the demonic forces will go. There is nothing left for them to feed on.

I fully recognize that depression in some people is a result of chemical imbalances. For these precious people the scripture in Acts 10:38 can have vivid meaning, how Jesus of Nazareth went about doing good, and healing all that were oppressed of the devil for God was with Him. The healing that Jesus bought by His own stripes before His cruel death on Calvary, can bring physical as well as chemical relief to those who suffer from depression. I have ministered healing to women who fell into depression because their hormones were changing during menopause. Others fell into depression when they had surgery. These cases required a healing in the same way those who were blind and lame required a healing. Jesus is perfectly able to heal for *"Jesus Christ is the same yesterday, today, and forever"* (Hebrews 13:8).

On the other hand, the majority of the cases of depression are rooted in emotional disturbances that produce wrong patterns of thinking. Depressed people are consumed with an oppressive thought life. I have also noted that depressed people are often consumed with thoughts of themselves. They rarely think of others and if they do, it is only to rehearse in their minds the wrongs done to them by others. Depression is very selfish.

King Saul offers a serious lesson on the results of unopposed oppression. Unopposed oppression leads to depression. Untreated depression leads to possession. Possession can lead to destruction and death. A person loses control and a demonic spirit begins to influence them. Their entire personality changes under this evil influence. Oppression resulting in depression will steal from your life and the lives of others around you, but it does not have to be so.

If you recognize you are suffering from depression, change your thoughts and change your life. Do you feel I have oversimplified that? Here is what I mean: do the opposite of what the enemy means for you to do. If you feel like going to bed, plant a flower instead. If you feel like withdrawing from people, call a friend and invite them to lunch. If you feel like holding a grudge and festering with anger, go to Jesus Christ and ask for forgiveness and offer forgiveness to the offended person. The fight through depression is challenging, but possible because of what Jesus Christ has won for us on the cross. Believers must accept and appropriate healing not only for their bodies, but also for their minds.

Depression can also be lessened or alleviated altogether by adopting a disciplined way of focusing on others instead of self. Learn to be compassionate toward others and the self-centeredness that often accompanies depression will disappear. There are many fruitful works for the Kingdom of God that places the focus on meeting others' needs. The Apostle James pointed us to this truth when he wrote, *"Pure and undefiled religion before God and the Father is this: to visit orphans and widows in their trouble, and to keep oneself unspotted from the world"* (James 1:27). Faith always requires action, even if you are a believer who suffers from depression. This kind of faith focuses on the needs of others.

Depression rooted in anger and rejection keeps many Christians from being free. Likely the enemy first flooded them with oppressive thoughts, getting them to gradually reduce the size of their God to the size of their problem. Next, the devil numbed them and caused them to suspend control of their active thinking processes. After that, he began to write on their blank slate thoughts that were not in accordance with the Word of God. Feelings of worthlessness wrapped up the whole mess in a dark blanket until the professing Christian couldn't or wouldn't even get out of bed. The focus was turned to them and their pain instead of the focus being on serving and honoring their Savior. King Saul descended quickly from oppression to depression and then possession by being self-focused. King David, however, constantly kept his focus on God. That kind of faith defeated depression and enlarged the Kingdom of God.

What you focus on will either lift your spirits, or cause you to be covered with a cloud of doubt and fear. Let your mind be stayed on the Lord and His Word. In order to keep yourself lifted above the problems you face, meditate on the scriptures, praise the Lord and make melody in your heart to Him! You must know that your God is bigger than your situation.

As you look back on what you have conquered, you can face the future with confidence and faith!